THE DEVELOPING CHILD

Bringing together and illuminating the remarkable recent research on development from infancy to adolescence, for students of developmental psychology, policy makers, parents, and all others concerned with the future of the next generation.

Series Editors

Jerome Bruner
New York University

Michael Cole
University of California, San Diego

Annette Karmiloff-Smith
Neurocognitive Development Unit,
Institute of Child Health, London

CHILDREN
OF IMMIGRATION

Carola Suárez-Orozco
Marcelo M. Suárez-Orozco

HARVARD UNIVERSITY PRESS
Cambridge, Massachusetts, and London, England

First Harvard University Press paperback edition, 2002

Library of Congress Cataloging-in-Publication Data

Suárez-Orozco, Carola, 1957–
Children of immigration / Carola Suárez-Orozco and Marcelo M. Suárez-Orozco.
   p. cm. — (The developing child)
Includes bibliographical references and index.
ISBN 0-674-00492-2 (cloth)
ISBN 0-674-00838-3 (pbk.)
1. Children of immigrants—United States. I. Suárez-Orozco, Marcelo M., 1956–
II. Title. III. Series.

HQ792.U5 S83 2001
305.23'0973—dc21   00-046129

CONTENTS

ACKNOWLEDGMENTS

While we are the sole "parents" of this book, many members of our "extended family" have been involved in its delivery and upbringing. It is a treat for us to thank all of the individuals and institutions that have so generously supported us during this project.

First and foremost, we would like to thank our immigrant informants—the children, their parents and relatives, and their friends. Over the years, they trusted us by opening their lives to us; in turn, we have tried to be faithful in relating their stories. Without them there would be no story to tell. These children and families brave discouraging odds in search of a better tomorrow. May their drive and faith be an example to us all—and may their new country live up to the challenge of harnessing their energies.

Families can thrive when they have generous godparents. We have been blessed by funding from ours—the W. T. Grant Foundation, the Spencer Foundation, and the National Science Foundation. Without their essential support we would have had a much less rich story to tell.

The main function of the family is the transfer of skills, values, and worldviews to the next generation. Other than the moving stories that immigrant children told us during our research, nothing has been more gratifying than to work with an extraordinarily talented group of young researchers who have been involved in various capacities with the Harvard Immigration Project. These research assistants have been our eyes and ears into immigrant homes, schools, and neighborhoods. Over the years, we have been stimulated by their penetrating insights, eager to hear the priceless vignettes they could not wait to share, and disheartened by some of what they encountered. They have kept us grounded and honest with the freshness and fearlessness of their gaze. Their intellectual integrity and humanistic commitment to the communities in which they work has been an invaluable gift. Those working with us at the time of the writing of this book are Jeannette Adames, Laura Alamillo, Lilian Bobea, Marco Bravo, Carmina Brittain, Alix Cantave, Sophia Cantave, Alexandra Celestin, Valerie Chanlot, Jennifer Chen, Dafney Dabach, Charlene Desir, Celeste Gutíerrez, Teresa Huerta, Iris Siu-Wai Hui, Jill Jefferis, Yih-Shiuan Liang, Mónica López, Julia Macias, Marcela Nazzari, Mariela Paez, Claudia Piñeda, Desiree Qin-Hilliard, Breca Rodriguez-Griswold, Leah Rosenbloom, Eliane Rubinstein-Avila, Irina Todovova, Peichi Tung, Yu-Mui Cecilia Wan, and Rebeca Zichlin. Those who have participated in the project in the past in various capacities include Consuelo Aceves, Esther Adames, QunWei Ai, Rosa Armendáriz, Joelle Berthelot, Linda Caswell, Virginia Chan, Nhi Chau, Sonya Contero, Yohanni Cuevas, Emmanuel Daphnis, Elsa Garcia, Sarah Hughes, Norma Jimenez, Rachel Kline, Marlene Losier, Josephine Louie, Nurys de Oleo-Park, Regine Ostine, Debra Rodman, Griselda Santiago, Eric Shaw, Zuwei Shi, Liz Vazquez, and Claire White. While every one of the research assistants has had something important to contribute to this project, Carmina, Charlene, Eliane, Jill, Mariela, and Yu-Mui have been centrally involved in nearly every aspect of the research: conceptually, methodologically, and in the field. It has been an honor to work with you all.

We also would like to say a special thank you to the members of our research support staff: Jennifer Hayes, Kimberly McGuffie, and Christina Nikitopoulos. While the research assistants have a good sense of what is going on in the sites they themselves are studying, Jennifer, Christina, and Kimberly have the big picture of the overall project. We have benefited from their counsel, especially when they have alerted us to similarities and discontinuities across sites. They are gracious, ever helpful, and more than once have performed exemplary work under the stress of impending deadlines.

A project of this magnitude can only be developed and sustained by the creative and intellectual efforts of a community of scholars. We are thankful to Terry Tivnan of the Harvard Graduate School of Education for his statistical and methodological guidance as well as his wonderful sense of humor.

In California, Curtis Vaughn has been responsible for managing our contingent of nearly a dozen graduate students from U.C. Berkeley, U.C. Davis, and elsewhere who have been working with us in the Mexican and Central American communities. We are grateful to Dr. Vaughn for the leadership and peace of mind he has afforded us.

Many senior colleagues from Harvard and elsewhere have lent their expertise to our project. Gary Orfield, Susan Moore-Johnson, Min Zhou, Paul Farmer, Sau Fong-Siu, Peggy Levitt, Alejandro Portes, George Spindler, and Mary Waters have all made presentations to the training seminar for our research assistants. We would like to especially thank Professor Waters for sending us an advance copy of her wonderful new book, *Black Identities*.

George De Vos, Celia Falicov, and John Ogbu have been mentors whose valuable insights have guided our development as scholars of immigration.

Kurt Fischer, Robert Levine, and Catherine Snow of the Harvard Graduate School of Education have steadily supported our research efforts since we made the move from California to Harvard.

John Coatsworth, director of Harvard's David Rockefeller Center for Latin American Studies, also welcomed us with a warm *abrazo* and provided us with wise counsel and much needed support, especially during the gestational period of this project.

Our dear Harvard colleague Doris Sommer has been a source of warmth and inspiration.

We would like to share our gratitude for the valuable feedback on portions of this book given by Maria Carlo and Sofia Villenas (both of Harvard University).

We are deeply indebted to June Erlick, publications director of the David Rockefeller Center for Latin American Studies, for many careful readings of versions of this manuscript. June is an exacting critic, a reader's reader, and a generous friend.

Marcela Nazzari provides our "home" during our regular monthly stays in California when we fly out to supervise the West Coast contingent of research assistants. She has long been our spiritual godparent.

Elizabeth Knoll, our editor at Harvard University Press, met with us at a critical point in the development of this book. Her vision and diplomacy shaped in many important ways the nature of this manuscript. Julie Carlson, our copyeditor, did a wonderful job of clarifying our academese and polishing our manuscript.

Finally, we would like to thank our "real" children, Marisa and Lucas. They have patiently participated in endless conversations at the dinner table, where between "How was your day?" "Pass the salad," and "More salsa please" the main topic of discussion seemed always to be immigration, immigration, immigration. Their love and sense of humor have been ever sustaining. *¡Gracias!*

CHILDREN OF IMMIGRATION

Large-scale immigration is one of the most important social developments of our time. It is a transformational process affecting families and their children. Once immigrants are settled, they send for their loved ones or form new families. Hence, the story of today's immigrants is also a saga of their children: a fascinating and critical—but too often forgotten—chapter of the immigrant experience. The children of immigrants, who make up 20 percent of all youth in the United States, are an integral part of the American fabric. This book explores their experiences.

First, a word about our use of the terms "immigrant children" and "children of immigrants." When we refer to immigrant children, we strictly mean foreign-born children who have migrated, not the U.S.-born second generation. "Children of immigrants," on the other hand, refers to both U.S.-born and foreign-born children. While the experiences of U.S.-born and foreign-born children differ in many respects (most importantly, all U.S.-born children are U.S. citizens), they nevertheless share an important common denominator: immigrant parents.

The children of immigrants follow many different pathways; they forge complex and multiply determined identities that resist easy generalizations. Some do extremely well in their new country. Indeed, research suggests that immigrant children are healthier, work harder in school, and have more positive social attitudes than their nonimmigrant peers.[1] Every year, the children of immigrants are overrepresented in the rosters of high school valedictorians and receive more of their share of prestigious science awards. They are regularly admitted to our most competitive elite universities. Immigrant children in general arrive with high aspirations and extremely positive attitudes toward education.

While we name and celebrate the hard-earned successes of many children of immigrants, there are reasons to worry about the long-term adaptations of others. Why should we worry? Because many children of immigrants today are enrolling in violent and overcrowded inner-city schools where they face overwhelmed teachers, hypersegregation by race and class, limited and outdated resources, and otherwise decaying infrastructures.[2] Disconcertingly high numbers of these children are leaving schools with few skills that would ensure success in today's unforgiving global economy. At a time when the U.S. economy is generating no meaningful jobs for high-school dropouts, many children of immigrants are dropping out of school. In brief, while many immigrant children succeed, others struggle to survive.

Anxiety has surged in recent years over the continued large-scale immigration into the United States. As in eras past, immigrants have been received with ambivalence. Though immigrant children arrive with remarkably positive social attitudes—toward schooling, authority figures, and the future—we argue in this book that their developing psyches are susceptible to the negative "social mirroring" that many experience in the new land. We contend that the immigrants' initial positive attitudes are a remarkable resource that must be cultivated. As a society we would be best served by harnessing those energies.

With more than 130 million migrants worldwide and a total foreign-born population of nearly 30 million people in the United States alone, immigration is rapidly transforming the postindustrial scene. In New York City schools, 48 percent of all students come from immigrant-headed households speaking more than one hundred different languages. In California, nearly 1.5 million children are classified as Limited English Proficient (LEP). This is not only an urban or southwestern phenomenon—schools across the country are encountering growing numbers of children from immigrant families. Even in places like Dodge City, Kansas, more than 30 percent of the children enrolled in public schools are the children of immigrants. To quote Dorothy in *The Wizard of Oz*, we are not in Kansas any more.

Discussions around immigration have typically concentrated on policy issues and, especially, the economy. With the exception of bilingual education, the debate about immigration—as well as much of the basic research—has focused predominantly on immigrant adults. Yet nationwide, "first and second generation immigrant children are the most rapidly growing segment of the U.S. child population."[3] The future character of American society and economy will be intimately related to the adaptations of the children of today's immigrants, even in the unlikely case of a drastic reduction of immigration in the coming decades.

A central theme of *Children of Immigration* is how the children of immigrants are faring in American society. What do we know about the children of immigrants? How does immigration affect the family system? How are the children adapting to our schools and making the transition to the workplace? We focus attention on their schooling because schools are where immigrant children first come into systematic contact with the new culture. Furthermore, adaptation to school is a significant predictor of a child's future well-being and contributions to society.

For the children of immigrants today, it is the best of times and the worst of times. In this book we explore the question of how it happens that while most immigrants enter the country with optimism and an energetic work ethic, many of their children are at risk of being marginalized and "locked out" of opportunities for a better tomorrow. Why will many immigrant children graduate from Ivy League colleges while others will end up in federal penitentiaries? For too many of the children of our most recent immigrants, the "Golden Door" of Emma Lazarus's classic poem is turning out to be more gilded than gold.

Exploring New Patterns of Immigration

Models developed over the past few decades to explain the immigrant experience in American society have been based largely on the European experience. Patterns of assimilation depicted a generally upwardly mobile journey; they foretold that the longer immigrants stayed in the United States, the better they would do in terms of schooling, health, and income. As Berkeley sociologist Robert Bellah once noted, "The United States was planned for progress," and each wave of immigrants was said to recapitulate this national destiny.

More recently, however, a number of distinguished social scientists have argued that a "segmentation" in the American economy and society is generating new patterns of immigrant insertion into American culture.[4] Factors such as race and color, parental education and socioeconomic status, racism, and interactions with other ethnic minority groups work together to shape the new immigrant's journey to and experience in the United States.[5] Today some new immigrants are progressing up the socioeconomic ladder at a rate never before seen in the history of U.S. immigration. Other newcomers may be getting locked out of the opportunity structure—in effect creating what some have termed a "rainbow underclass."[6] The children of these immigrants, not surprisingly, are at risk of achieving less than their native-born peers in terms of grades, performance in standardized tests, and attitudes toward education. They are also at risk of having a higher dropout rate.[7]

Furthermore, several scholars from different disciplines and using a variety of methods have identified another disconcerting phenomenon. For many immigrant groups, length of residency in the United States is associated with declining health, school achievement, and aspirations.[8] A recent large-scale National Research Council (NRC) study considered a variety of measures of physical health and risk behaviors among children and adolescents from immigrant families—including general health, learning disabilities, obesity, emotional difficulties, and risk behaviors. These NRC researchers found that immigrant youth were healthier than their counterparts from nonimmigrant families. These findings are "counterintuitive in light of the minority status, overall lower socio-economic status, and higher poverty rates that characterize many immigrant children and families." The NRC study also found that the longer that immigrant youth remain in the United States, the poorer their overall physical and psychological health. Furthermore, the more "Americanized" they became, the more likely they were to engage in risky behaviors such as substance abuse, unprotected sex, and delinquency.[9]

In the area of education, sociologists Rubén Rumbaut and Alejandro Portes surveyed more than 5,000 high school students in San Diego, California, and Dade County, Florida.[10] They conclude that "an important finding supporting our earlier reported research is the *negative* association of length of residence in the United States with both GPA and aspirations. Time in the United States is, as expected, strongly predictive of improved English reading skills; but despite that seeming advantage, longer residence in the U.S. and second generation status [that is, being born in the United States] are connected to declining academic achievement and aspirations, net of other factors."[11] In a different voice, Reverend Virgil Elizondo, rector of the San Fernando Cathedral in San Antonio, Texas, articulates this same problem: "I can tell by looking in their eyes how long they've been here. They come sparkling with hope, and the first generation finds hope rewarded. Their children's eyes no longer sparkle."[12]

A number of social scientists have explored the issues of variability and decline in the academic performance and social adaptation of immigrant children. Several factors have been implicated. Social scientists have argued that the "capital" that the immigrant families bring with them—including financial resources, social class and educational background, psychological and physical health, as well as social supports—have a clear influence on the immigrant experience. Legal status, race, color, and language also mediate how children adapt to the upheavals of immigration. Economic opportunities and neighborhood characteristics—including the quality of schools where immigrants settle, racial and class segregation, neighborhood decay, and violence—all contribute significantly to the adaptation process. Anti-immigrant sentiment and racism also play a role. These factors combine in ways that lead to very different outcomes.

In this book we take a new, interdisciplinary perspective: we consider historical as well as contemporary social attitudes, opportunities, and barriers. We also examine in some detail the psychosocial experiences of immigration and consider how these factors may interact in ways that lead to divergent pathways of adaptation and identity formation.

Immigration typically results in substantial gains for the people who move. Some immigrants escape political, religious, or ethnic persecution, while others migrate for economic reasons. Long-separated families may be reunited. Some immigrants are motivated by the opportunity for social mobility, while others migrate in the spirit of adventure. Though immigration is a highly stressful process, for many, immigration is worth the sacrifices. But the gains of immigration come at a considerable cost.

Immigrant families profoundly feel the pressures of migration. Immigration can destabilize family life in a variety of ways. New data from the Harvard Immigration Project suggest that the immigrant journey into the United States is a highly fractured, phase-specific process that results in psychosocially complex patterns of family fragmentation and reunification. Children are often left behind in the country of origin in the care of grandparents or other relatives. In other cases, the children are sent ahead to the United States to stay with distant relatives while the rest of the family prepares for their own migration. Often it is years before the nuclear family is reunited. In this book, we examine the psychosocial processes involved in these patterns of entry into American society.

We also explore the Faustian bargain that every immigrant parent makes: although many immigrant parents are motivated by a desire for a better future for their children, the very process of immigration tends to undermine parental authority and family cohesion. A common fear for immigrant parents is to "lose" their children to the new culture. We consider the seductive draw of the more acculturated peer group that often works to undermine the parental voice. In these pages, we recognize how vitally important to the children's successful adaptation are the parents' ability to maintain respect for family and the child's connection to the culture of origin. Our data suggest that those children whose parents maintain a voice of authority while encouraging them to achieve what we term "bicultural competencies" will be best placed to take full advantages of the opportunities available.

Immigrant children undergo a particular constellation of changes and experiences likely to influence their developing psyches. We examine how the ambivalent reception that many encounter exacerbates the stresses of immigration. We also develop a theoretical framework around the concept of "social mirroring" to explore how the children of immigrants come to craft their identities in part as a function of how they are viewed and received by the dominant culture. Immigration can become traumatic for children when anti-immigrant disparagement and discrimination, as well as structural barriers, add to the already stressful nature of immigration. How does a child incorporate the notion that she is an alien, or an illegal—that she is unwanted and does not warrant the most basic rights of education and health care?

In the United States, the history of anti-immigrant sentiment is as long as the history of immigration itself. Today, this sentiment appears to endure as a "last frontier" in which citizens openly vent racial and ethnic hostilities. While blatant racism is largely confined to the fringes of society, anti-immigrant sentiments are more freely indulged in public opinion, policy debates, and other social forums. Even children articulate anti-immigrant feelings. Students in a public high school in Northern California had these thoughts to share with educational researcher Laurie Olsen: "They come to take our jobs, and are willing to break their backs . . . and we can't compete." Another said, "These Chinese kids come over here and all they do is work and work and work and work, and all you have to do is look in the AP classes and you'll see they are filling them up. No one can compete any more." Still another summed up a prevailing fear: "They just want to take over."[13]

Whether seen as high-achieving book-obsessed competitors or as lazy and prone to violence, immigrant children are subjected to a variety of stereotypes. Immigrant groups who are highly visible because of their race, color, and language are typically singled out for culturally elaborate and sometimes debilitating stereotypes. Some immigrants, such as Canadians and Irish, are less visible now and not currently considered to be a problem or threat. Other immigrants tend to elicit anxieties that lead to stereotypes of sinister and cunning people working behind the scenes to manipulate the economy and the social structure of their new country. This stereotype, for example, has affected both Jews and Asians.

Today's immigrants of color are seen by many as possessing traits that make them "unmeltable" and incompatible with modern American culture. Like other minority groups (such as African Americans and Puerto Ricans), some new immigrants have been characterized as being culturally inferior, lazy, and prone to crime, and therefore less deserving of sharing in the dreams of dominant mainstream society. We examine how such negative "social mirroring" has corrosive effects on children's developing sense of self. We present new data from our study of recent immigrant children that highlight their sensitivity to these attitudes. We argue that in facing such forms of symbolic violence, some immigrant minority children experience the institutions of the mainstream society—such as its schools—as foreign and hostile communities that reproduce the order of inequality. We also explore how a culture of institutional distrust leads many disparaged immigrant students to turn away from school as an avenue for getting ahead.

Immigrant parents often see themselves as better off than they were in the old country. They also frequently view the United States as a great source of opportunity for a better future. Many children of immigrants are able to maintain the same positive momentum, energy, and faith in a better tomorrow that led their parents to move in the first place. Others, especially those who no longer compare their current lives with what they left behind but instead look to the majority culture as the standard, may come to experience their circumstances in the new country as one of deprivation and marginality. In short, while some children of immigrants come to see immigration as a journey fraught with discrimination and economic difficulties, others experience the journey as one of hope and opportunity.

A Study from Many Points of View

In this book we bring multiple perspectives to our understanding of these issues. Carola Suárez-Orozco—an "old immigrant" from Europe—is a cultural psychologist in Human Development and Psychology at the Harvard Graduate School of Education with nearly two decades of experience working in a variety of contexts with immigrant families and children. Marcelo Suárez-Orozco—a "new immigrant" from Latin America—is an anthropologist who teaches Human Development at the Harvard Graduate School of Education. His life's work has been the comparative study of immigration. Over the last two decades our research has attempted to capture the voices of immigrant and second-generation children living in the United States and other parts of the world.

Together we codirect the Harvard Immigration Project, and our most recent research with newcomers from Central America, China, the Dominican Republic, Haiti, and Mexico has provided us with a unique comparative perspective into immigrant children's lives. The Longitudinal Immigrant Student Adaptation study (LISA) began in the fall of 1997 as a major research initiative of the newly established Harvard Immigration Project. With funding from the National Science Foundation, the W. T. Grant Foundation, and the Spencer Foundation, this research is tracking over time the experiences of more than four hundred recently arrived children of immigrants enrolled in over fifty schools in the Boston and San Francisco areas.[14]

Most research on the children of immigrants confounds generational status, lumping together newly arrived immigrants, first-generation, second-generation, and even third-generation children in a single category. We believe that this is a major methodological flaw. The experiences of recently arrived immigrants, we suggest, are in some ways unique and must be analytically isolated from issues facing the subsequent U.S.-born generations.[15] Therefore, our study had strict criteria for participation.[16] LISA participants are all youth born abroad who recently arrived in the United States.

We employ a variety of social science techniques that include structured questionnaires of children, their parents and teachers, ethnographic fieldwork in their schools and communities, and psychological and narrative techniques. We also make use of achievement tests as well as a variety of data collected by the participating schools, such as grades, attendance records, and disciplinary actions.

A team of thirty research assistants (RAs) is conducting the fieldwork and interviews for the LISA project. The researchers embody the energy, brilliance, and work ethic that is the best immigrants have to offer. Most are immigrants or the children of immigrants. They are all graduate-trained scholars with substantial research and personal interests in the field of immigration. Most are advanced graduate students at Harvard, the University of California at Berkeley, University of California at Davis, Boston University, Tufts, and other leading research universities. This team is unique because its members are at once members of the communities they are studying as well as trained social scientists deeply concerned with the accurate description and interpretation of the immigrant experience. They work in schools and communities that typify the settings toward which immigrants gravitate. Some are working in excellent schools with cutting-edge curricula, charismatic administrators, and enthusiastic teachers. Others are working in schools that can best be characterized as "war zones"—schools where bombings, stabbings, and shootings have occurred during the course of our research.

In designing our basic research, we have borrowed tools from a variety of social science disciplines. We have found that survey-like and structured questionnaires, typically used by research sociologists, are quite useful for detecting broad group differences. But these survey-style questionnaires are not enough. In conducting our research, we discovered that many survey-type questions are not really understood by immigrant children and even their parents. Social science interviewing is a cultural practice that is simply foreign to many immigrants, adults and children alike. A number of our RAs reported feeling that some children simply responded with "what they thought we wanted to hear." After years of basic research we concluded that survey-like data, by themselves, tend to suggest a distorted picture. What immigrant children say and what they do are often very different. _hard to study?_

Perhaps this is a limitation inherent in all self-reported data. For example, nearly all of the children reported in their responses to structured questionnaires that doing well in school was very important to them. Yet by observing the children in the schools—in the classrooms, playground, cafeteria, and elsewhere—we found that some children's behavior suggested different priorities. Through ethnography we learned about the immigrant boy who over time disengaged from schoolwork and gravitated toward the culture of the "backroom boys"—into an ethos of cutting school, missing homework, and generally viewing schoolwork as "boring." Yet all along he was telling us he will go to college "for a couple of years" to become a physician. _unrealistic expectations?_

Hence, we advocate ethnographic work in conjunction with structured questionnaires. The ethnographic process, based on the slow building of long-term interpersonal relations with the children in various social settings (schools, home, and neighborhoods) is critical to our understanding of their adaptations. Ethnographic observations sensitize us to the power of social context in shaping the lives of immigrant children. Ethnography also allows us to discover critical phenomena that we could not detect otherwise. While conducting her ethnographic fieldwork, one of our RAs discovered that immigrant parents pooled their limited resources to pay a teacher to conduct an after-school program of intense English and math tutoring. Thus we became aware of how some immigrant parents generate informal parallel structures—indeed create their own "phantom" schools—to aid in their children's learning. We might never have discovered this had we relied on structured interviews alone.

Ethnography has its clear limitations. There are the eternal problems with sampling and self-selection—ethnographies almost inevitably are centered on a handful of "key informants." The routine questions that ethnographers face include: How representative are the key informants? What should be done when informants disagree? Can one generalize from a handful of cases? More importantly, ethnographic descriptions of social and cultural phenomena can be deceptive if they fail to fully explore how informants "metabolize"—both take in and respond to—their experiences in a given social setting. Two children in the same setting will have completely different experiences. To push the metaphor further, "metabolic rates" are set by cultural expectations and psychological tendencies.

Simple observations and descriptions are not enough. We have been in schools that are, by any criteria, disaster areas: overcrowded, violence-ridden, and hampered by outdated curriculums. Yet more than once, our RAs were stunned and saddened when immigrant children, and indeed parents, told them that these schools were wonderful—a great step forward from what they had back home.

An easily agreed-upon "objective reality," such as a disaster-area school—a reality that we can observe, measure, analyze, and transform—often means something very different to a recently arrived immigrant than to a native citizen. There are, of course, no excuses for poorly functioning schools. No child should be exposed to the toxic social and educational environment of such schools. Yet we have learned that we cannot assume that an "objective reality" means the same to different actors. This is especially true of recent immigrants who frequently compare their current lot with the standards and expectations of their country of origin. And for many new immigrants coming from extremely poor countries, the advantages in the new land are obvious and self-evident. Yet middle-class immigrants are indeed as horrified as native middle-class citizens would be of conditions we found in many schools.

Ethnographic descriptions that stay at a superficial level nearly always produce distorted portraits. They typically fail to notice how the child experiences the world. Hence, in our research we have advocated the use of ethnography along with psychocultural tools that enable us to explore the changing inner motivations and interpersonal concerns of immigrant children. Without reference to the inner and interpersonal worlds, we cannot meaningfully consider issues of agency, consciousness, and empowerment—the very things that make us truly human. Human beings are not moved to act simply by impersonal social forces. This is especially true of immigrants who defy the odds by choosing to leave their places of birth and plotting a new course in a foreign land. Any study that fails to pay attention to complex psychocultural processes is at risk of missing much of the immigrant experience.

In this book, we draw on data from the first year of the LISA project as well as from more than twenty years of basic research and practice with immigrants, refugees, and second-generation children.[17] Likewise, we make use of immigrant memoirs, films, and plays that illuminate the varieties of experience among the children of immigrants. We also, of course, rely on the prior and ongoing research efforts of colleagues in a variety of disciplines. We seek to explore the emotional and psychosocial experience of immigration for children while considering the many social obstacles and opportunities in their way.

The book is designed to provide an overview of the major themes in the lives of the children of immigrants—the nature of their journey to the United States, their earliest perceptions, and their subsequent transformations. The book centers around children and their experiences.

This book can be read in a variety of ways by a variety of audiences. Practitioners working with children in school settings, health care settings, and social agencies will gain insight into the lives of the children that they strive to serve. Scholars in immigration studies, cultural psychology, and anthropology will find the book's interdisciplinary perspective of relevance. While the book coheres best when read in its entirety, each chapter can stand alone.

In Chapter 1, we explore the various pathways that immigrant families take to their new homes. We draw a distinction between "immigrants," "transnationals," and "refugees."

In Chapter 2, we ask a basic question: What is *new* about the "new immigration"? We examine in some detail how the "new immigration" differs from the "old immigration" of one hundred years ago. We discuss historical responses to immigration and examine the parallels to current dynamics. And we briefly examine some of the recurring concerns about today's immigrants and present a series of findings that place the concerns in perspective.

In Chapter 3, we turn to the psychosocial effects of immigration on families and children. We examine the gains and losses that come about with immigration. We explore how families manage the psychosocial tensions created by the separations and reunifications of migration. We consider the changes, opportunities, and stresses in family dynamics, including new roles for immigrant children, "social demotions," parent-child role reversals, and the remaking of gender relations.

In Chapter 4, we discuss how the children of immigrants reformulate their identities in the new society. In this chapter we introduce the concept of "social mirroring." We provide evidence of children's sensitivity to perceptions and expectations of them found in today's ethos of reception. The all-too-often distorted reflections, we argue, have a corrosive effect on the developing identities of children. In this chapter we also explore the dual frame of reference through which immigrants filter their experiences. We ask whether immigrant parents' constant comparisons of the "here and now" with the "there and then" holds less relevance for their children—especially as the children encounter hostile attitudes and discrimination. We consider the centripetal forces drawing children of immigrants toward the multiple cultural fields in which they find themselves. We examine the social process of marginalization that shape the experience of many immigrants of color today. And we describe three styles of identity development common to children of immigrants, illustrating them with case studies that bring these theoretical descriptions to life.

In Chapter 5, the concluding chapter, we discuss the factors that seem to contribute to divergent pathways of school adaptation among immigrant children today. Schools are the great sites of cultural contact between new arrivals and more established citizens.

What happens in schools today will to a large degree determine the future of all of our children.

In the Epilogue we reflect on the idea of acculturation. The seminal empirical and theoretical work on immigrant acculturation is based on the great wave of European immigration to the United States, which climaxed in the earlier part of this century.[18] Is this paradigm for acculturation still relevant?

1

THE VARIETIES OF
IMMIGRANT EXPERIENCE

Mei was born in an exclusive neighborhood in Hong Kong.[1] Her parents were focused in their motivation for migrating to the United States. As her mother put it, the family moved "to provide our children with a better learning environment." The parents were concerned that in Hong Kong students like Mei and her brother, Xi, felt too much pressure to prepare for brutally competitive exams that are used to exclude even excellent students from pursuing higher education.

Mei, her parents, and her brother, Xi, came to Boston to visit relatives one summer a few years ago. After some reflection, the parents decided that Xi would stay behind with an aunt and uncle in a Boston suburb to pursue his high school studies. The parents returned to Hong Kong with Mei to prepare the family to make the permanent move. The family arrived in the United States nine months after receiving the proper documentation from the Immigration and Naturalization Service (INS). Three years after their migration, her mother was working as a Head Start teacher while her father had joined a high-tech company as a software engineer. Like many other immigrants, Mei's father had a second job (in the PC-board import business).

Mei is a stellar student who is well liked by both peers and teachers. She has mastered the English language and already finds herself struggling to find words in her native Cantonese. Her mother is concerned that Mei's new school is "too easy."

Ramon's mother revealed poignantly why she immigrated to the

United States from El Salvador: "I came to save my life. My husband was in the military. He wanted to get out, so they tortured him and then he 'disappeared.' Then they came looking for me so I came here illegally to escape." When his mother was forced to leave almost overnight, Ramon, a sad-eyed and slightly overweight twelve-year-old, stayed behind with caring relatives. He was able to join his mother after three years of separation.

When asked to complete the sentence "In life the most important thing is . . . " Ramon promptly responded: "my school." His mother reports with some irony in her voice that she is now forced to keep Ramon indoors after school and on weekends because of the pervasive violence and drug-related activities in their neighborhood. Though his friends and neighbors are nearly all Spanish speaking from a variety of countries (including El Salvador, Guatemala, and Mexico), Ramon spends most of his time indoors watching TV in English. In school, he is well behaved but struggles academically. One of his teachers wonders whether he is depressed or perhaps has a learning disability.

Monica, a vivacious ten-year-old with a warm smile and deeply inquiring eyes, arrived in the San Francisco area two years ago. Born in a Mexican border town with a booming tourist industry, she followed in the footsteps of her mother, who had migrated there three years earlier to learn English. When asked how she fared during the extended separation from her mother, Monica seemed puzzled because, she said, her mother had kept in close contact, visiting her often and regularly sending her gifts.

Monica's mother was anxious that her three children learn English because, as she put it, "it is the universal language." Her children, she insisted, will all become professionals. "We came here to go forward, not backward," she reasoned. Her dream was that her children, with their flawless English and American education, would one day thrive in the upper levels of the tourist industry "either here [in the United States] or there [in Mexico]."

Monica loves her new school. When asked to complete the sentence "School is . . . " her immediate response was "the pathway to success." She excels in soccer and karate. Her teachers noted that

Monica's progress in English was remarkable. Though she greatly values her newly acquired language, Monica's loyalty to her native Spanish is obvious. She says, with condemnation in her voice, that Latino students who no longer speak Spanish "negate Mexico." While she loves her new school and is thriving academically, her loyalties to Mexico run deep. Nearly every holiday the family, en masse, returns to the border town where the children were born and where all their relatives live.

When asked why his family decided to migrate to Boston, André, a soft-spoken but precociously dignified twelve-year-old, replied chillingly, "There was too much killing in Haiti." While his father's explanation was more complex, it conveyed the same message. "Peace" in the United States was a primary factor in the decision to migrate, his father said. The father elaborated that beyond the safety concerns, he had been motivated by the economic opportunities and schooling options available to his children in the United States. He articulates the essence of the immigrant's project: "I wanted a better life for my wife and children."

André's father was the family's migration pioneer. He came to the United States six years ago, leaving his wife and children in a violence-torn neighborhood in Haiti's capital. Though college educated, André's father had to make a living as he could—mostly as a janitor and in maintenance work. Though demoralized by his inability to find work commensurate with his skill level, he worked regularly and was able to send money to his family in Haiti every month.

After a separation of over four years, André was able to join the father he now barely knew. His mother remained in Haiti, caring for the loving grandmother André dearly misses. André is enrolled in a bilingual program where he has little contact with white American children. Nevertheless, he is making good progress with his English. He hopes to one day become a doctor.

Sergio is a shy and acutely self-conscious twelve-year-old who arrived from a small rural village in Guatemala just over a year ago. He speaks Mayan as his first language and Spanish as his second. Sergio was left behind in Guatemala with his grandparents for six years. His father, mother, and uncles had gone ahead on the dangerous journey north by land through Mexico. They sent for Sergio once they felt secure enough to bring their son into the country. His parents said that in rural Guatemala there was nothing for them to do, "no jobs, no opportunities, no future."

In Sergio's view, the hardest thing about immigration for the family was being apart for so long. In response to the question "What do you hope for your family?" he responded, "that we will always be together." Though he is delighted to be reunited with his parents, he deeply misses his grandmother, cousins, and classmates in Guatemala.

Sergio told us that the best thing about living in the United States was "having shoes and a telephone." He is now enrolled in a San Francisco Bay Area school where most of his classmates are Mexican. While he interacts in Spanish with his Mexican peers, he does not feel fully accepted by them. His teachers find him to be well behaved and highly motivated to learn English.

As these portraits suggest, multiple pathways structure the immigrant's journeys into their new home. Many children of immigrants enter the United States because their families are fleeing economic or political insecurity. Others come not simply to survive, but rather to thrive by taking full advantage of economic and professional opportunities. For analytical purposes, the motivations can be divided into two broad categories: socioeconomic factors and factors relating to fear of persecution based on political, ethnic, and religious affiliations.[2] In the real lives of real migrants, however, the pathways are not always so distinct. More often than not, the family's decision is motivated by a variety of factors. Nevertheless, these categories are useful for understanding the experiences of immigrant families and their children.

In general, we call those who leave voluntarily due to social and economic motivations "immigrants," while those who are escaping to freedom (paraphrasing Erich Fromm) we call "asylum seekers" or "refugees." While they differ significantly in many important ways, immigrants and asylum seekers also share a number of common characteristics.

Once settled, both immigrants and asylum seekers often seek to bring family members to join them. A powerful (and natural) centripetal force draws families together. Indeed, over the last four decades, family reunification has continued to significantly add to the pool of new arrivals in American society.

Both asylum seekers and immigrants can have either documented ("legal") or undocumented ("illegal") status in their new country. In fact, contrary to widely held beliefs; the vast majority of immigrants in the United States today are documented.[3] Many others remain in a limbo status (sometimes for many years) while their documentation requests are being considered and processed by the INS. The majority of asylum seekers fail to gain official (legal) status as formal refugees—with all the rights and obligations that such status confers.[4]

It would be a mistake to assume that asylum seekers and immigrants are internally homogeneous groups. For example, asylum seekers can be upper-status political elites (such as the early wave of Cuban refugees in Miami), members of an oppressed ethnic group (such as the Kosovo Albanians), or the poor and disenfranchised (such as those arriving from Haiti escaping state terrorism). Likewise, immigrants have highly personal motivations. Some seek to permanently settle in the new land. Others intend to return home eventually and view themselves as sojourners or temporary transnational migrants.

Immigrant Pathways

Immigration, a major life decision, has important psychological and social implications for the individual and the family group. On the eve of departure, immigrants face an uncertain future with potential for both gains and losses. It is an enterprise that is often carefully planned and never taken lightly.

Throughout human history, immigrants have been driven by twin forces: powerful socioeconomic factors as well as individual agency and motivation. What makes people migrate? Scholars of immigration have very different views.

Economists, not surprisingly, tend to emphasize factors such as employment and wages. Thus, in their view, a would-be immigrant from rural China makes a rational cost-benefit calculation that migrating to the United States will result in substantial gains for himself and his family. For example, he may conclude that in a month of working two or three jobs in the United States, he can earn more than he would in a year in China.

Economists talk about "push" factors—including unemployment, underemployment, and differences in wages between countries—and the "pull" factors such as employers' recruitment of immigrant workers.[5] In many settings, international labor-recruiting networks deliver low-skilled foreign workers into low-paying, physically demanding, and dangerous jobs that locals find unappealing.[6] Employers seek these immigrants because they are noted for being compliant, reliable, and flexible about their job duties and hours.[7]

While some wonder if an advanced postindustrial economy like that of the United States really still needs to rely on foreign-born workers, other researchers argue that foreign workers continue to be critical to vast sectors of the U.S. economy.[8] Large agricultural firms in dusty California towns—"agrobusiness"—are no longer alone in their strident lobbying for immigrant workers; the high-tech industry has joined the clamor. Indeed, in the last decade, the voracious demand for immigrant labor continues to draw workers from other countries.

On the other hand, sociologists tend to look for the causes of immigration in interpersonal forces and social networks. People migrate because others—relatives, friends, and friends of friends—migrated before them. The first immigrants break the ground for the foundation in the new land. They provide connections that are vital to subsequent immigrants from the same point of origin, by collecting information and contacts about jobs, places to live, schools, and so forth. Over time, powerful self-sustaining transnational networks are generated. It is no accident, then, that one of our research sites, in the largely Dominican Boston neighborhood of Jamaica Plain, has been dubbed "Baní Plain" after the Dominican town of Baní where many residents have their roots.

Another group of immigration observers—anthropologists—

tend to focus on the cultural reasons behind immigration. Changes in cultural models about what is a desirable standard of living have figured powerfully in the history of immigration. When would-be immigrants see television images and hear first-hand accounts of life abroad, they begin to imagine a better future in another social setting. The media, increasingly a telescopic acculturation force, combine with an informal network of reported immigration experiences to extend the possibilities for new social and economic horizons. The search for a better standard of living is an enduring motivation among immigrants from such varied places as Ireland (en route to Boston), Japan (en route to Sao Paulo), and China (en route to San Francisco).

In certain cultural groups, immigration is seen as a rite of passage: when young men and women come of age, they are expected to migrate. In some rural Mexican towns, for example, a stunningly high proportion of youth migrate after reaching a certain age. Many never return; instead they start families in their new land.[9]

Immigrant parents share with other parents back home attitudes about the opportunities available to the next generation in the new country. During the course of our research, immigrant parents often reported that a primary motivation for leaving was to pursue better opportunities for their children in the new country.

These attitudes seem to change and intensify after parents settle in the new country and begin to have a better sense of the formidable task ahead. Many times they are faced with a severe social demotion. Old skills and degrees do not easily translate into good jobs in the new country. Luís Rodríguez, in his devastating memoir, describes how his father, a proud Mexican science teacher, ends up working as a lab janitor in Southern California.[10] This is not uncommon. A Chinese doctor ends up working as a hospital attendant, and a Romanian photojournalist becomes a maid in a bed and breakfast.[11] Indeed, many of the parents in our study reported that while they were making more money than they had in their countries of origin, their social status was lower. Age, language skill, accreditation, and the enormous pressures to support the family financially (family both here and there) sharply limit the opportunities of many immigrant parents.

As these realities begin to sink in, the dream that their children may have a better future comes to sustain the parents. Our data suggest that prior to immigration (and indeed in the first phases of immigrant settlement in the new land), many parents have somewhat vague notions about "better opportunities," a "better life," or routes to "financial success" in the new country. Over time, and as they become keen observers of their new homeland, many immigrant parents begin to focus sharply on their children's education and schooling as the key to a better tomorrow. The belief that their children will have greater educational opportunities (and hence a better future) makes their sacrifices worthwhile.

Immigration involves economic, social, *and* cultural factors, and thus its totality cannot be reduced to a single variable. The case of Maria and her family illustrates the complexities that characterize the process of immigration as it plays out in everyday life.

Maria was a teacher in her native Guatemala and her husband, Pedro, was a charismatic labor organizer who rose through the union ranks to a position of prominence in their community. As the violence intensified in Guatemala during the 1980s, Maria and Pedro worried about their safety, as well as their own and their children's future. In letters from a cousin in the San Francisco Bay Area (who had moved there several years earlier), Maria learned of what seemed like a vastly improved quality of life. Maria's cousin told her of her color television, stereo system, car, and the free education for children. Maria's cousin also offered her a job in her growing business of cleaning houses in the Bay Area. Furthermore, she mentioned that her husband's boss frequently asked if he knew of other hard workers who needed jobs—hence the possibility for a well-paying construction job for Pedro.

From their small town in Guatemala, these opportunities (and the dollar figures attached to their job prospects) became irresistible, especially after Pedro began receiving death threats for his union activities. The more she communicated with her cousin in San Fran-

had good jobs there came here & had low jobs

cisco, the more Maria began to envision a brighter and safer future with a much higher standard of living. Eventually, the delicate dance between "pull and push" brought them to the Mission District, an ethnic Latino neighborhood in urban San Francisco. Jobs were readily available, as they had been promised. While the pay was excellent relative to what they were used to (their combined income quadrupled), they found it more demoralizing than they anticipated to have jobs with lower social status: Maria worked as a maid and Pedro had a construction job. They also found that life in the United States was quite expensive, which required them to work long hours and in several jobs. Most upsetting was their realization, nearly a year after their arrival, that with their very limited English skills it would be impossible for them to find work more commensurate with their education and skills. A depressing sense that their lives would be characterized by hard physical labor was tolerable only because they could see their son begin to flourish in his new school. Their son Jorge was learning English quickly and was well liked by his teachers, who saw him as a bright, polite, and hard-working student. Over time, as his English skills developed, Jorge became the family's main interlocutor with the outside world. Eventually, a supportive school counselor approached his parents telling them that Jorge would be an ideal candidate for college.

Today in the United States and many other postindustrial economies, foreign-born workers (both the highly skilled as well as the low-skilled) do not travel solo. They come with their families or over time form families in their new land. Immigrants have much to gain by moving to a new land, and business and industry have much to gain from immigrant labor. It is an illusion, however, to think that there are no costs associated with large-scale immigration—there clearly are. Immigrants need a variety of services, perhaps most importantly education for their children.[12] In the long term, it is hypocritical and indeed self-destructive for a society that depends on immigrant workers to not support these workers' aim of becoming full contributors to that society.

In recent years, a perverse pattern has become evident: those who have the most to gain by large-scale immigration (businesses), do not necessarily contribute a fair share to the services that the new arrivals will need. And taxpayers, who benefit more indirectly from immigration, often feel burdened by having to "pay the bills" for educating and providing health care and other services to immigrants and their families. The tension between the employers' interests and the reality that immigrant workers come as "package deals" with human needs provides fodder for the immigration debate. But as long as there is a voracious demand for immigrant labor, immigrant children will be seen in growing numbers in our schools, neighborhoods, and parks.

Refugee Pathways

When Sigmund Freud was asked late in life to give his formula for a happy life, his interlocutor surely expected a long and complex answer. Instead, Freud spontaneously replied with his famous one-liner: "To be able to love and work." The good Viennese doctor would be delighted to know that "love and work" also factor mightily as a force in human migration. Indeed, we have a reasonable understanding of how the twin forces of "love" (family reunification) and "work" structure international migration. On the other hand, the role of war and its relations to large-scale migratory flows have been generally neglected, even though throughout history war and migration have been closely linked.

The Cold War both deterred immigration—because of strict Iron Curtain controls—and generated large population displacements. The robust Cuban diaspora in the United States can be traced almost directly to tensions between the former Soviet Union and the United States.[13] Low-intensity warfare in Central America during the 1980s generated unprecedented population displacements. As a result, there are now well over a million Central Americans in the United States, most of whom sought asylum after 1980.[14] In the 1990s, ongoing conflicts in the former Yugoslavia drove large numbers of asylum seekers from the Balkans into Europe and the United States.

Asylum seekers are those escaping a country because of, in the words of the Geneva Convention of 1951, "a well-founded fear of persecution." State bureaucrats use complex formulas for deciding who is formally admitted as a "refugee"—with all the rights and obligations that status entitles under international law.

In the post–Cold War era, there has been an explosive growth in the numbers of asylum seekers worldwide. For example, some 369,000 foreigners requested asylum in Europe during 1998. In 1997, the United States registered a total of 112,158 refugees and asylum seekers. Only a small fraction of those seeking asylum are eventually granted formal refugee status.

In recent years, the United States and many other postindustrial nations such as Germany, France, and Belgium have developed new strategies to deal with increasing numbers of asylum seekers.[15] For example, the 13,000 Kosovars that arrived in Germany in mid-1999 were given a three-month renewable "Temporary Protective Status" on the condition that they *not* apply for refugee status—in effect, they forfeited the rights and entitlements that come with formal refugee status. Similar arrangements were made for asylum seekers from Bosnia and, earlier, for Salvadorians in the United States.

In the face of growing numbers of asylum seekers, and a widespread public concern that many of them are "economic refugees" in search of a better life in wealthier countries, new formal and informal strategies have been put into place. Many of these new strategies seem designed to prevent asylum seekers from accessing "safe countries"—where, under Geneva Convention agreements, they would have the right to a "fair hearing."

The high-seas interdiction program put into effect in the United States in the early 1990s is an example. The strategy was conceived to prevent large numbers of Haitian (and more recently Cuban) asylum seekers from arriving in U.S. territory—or even within its territorial waters—where they could establish certain legal protections. When they are apprehended in international waters and returned them to their country, asylum seekers are left with little practical recourse under international law. In mid-1999, this strategy came into public view and generated some embarrassment for the INS. U.S. television footage showed Coast Guard agents employing pepper mace and fire hoses in an attempt to prevent a small group of Cuban "boat people" from reaching U.S. land.[16]

Asylum seekers today must navigate increasingly turbulent legal waters. Those who succeed may eventually gain formal protections and rights and can begin their lives in the new country. Those who are rejected are often returned to their countries of origin or to a third "safe country." Still others may be held in detention camps pending deportation. In some cases, people—including children— linger for years in INS detention camps and jails because their country of birth refuses to take them back.[17] In other cases, as the odds have turned against them, those escaping persecution at home simply do not apply for asylum. Rather, they enter the country illegally and "disappear" into the shadowy world of undocumented immigration. We will return to the issue of undocumented immigration later in this chapter.

The most fundamental difference between an immigrant and an asylum seeker is the motivation for migration. Whereas migrants more or less voluntarily choose to move, asylum seekers are by definition involuntary newcomers. This fact has several important implications for the adaptations of families and children. Typically, those seeking asylum cannot carefully plan their move in the way that most immigrants do. Often, when the threats become imminent, families must make the move at once. Elaborate preparations, including the psychologically critical work of imagining life in the new country, are impossible.

The sudden and involuntary nature of the process generates tremendous tensions within the family. Parents must leave their country because they can no longer discharge the most basic of all parental functions: to provide for the safety and well-being of the children. In some cases, refugee children are victims (or witnesses) of war-related violence.[18] Many eventually show signs of having post-traumatic stress syndrome.

This situation may create within the family feelings of failure, guilt, and remorse. Families are typically separated—for example, a parent might suddenly need to go into hiding. In many cases, one parent must leave the country ahead of the rest, in the hope that the family will reunite later. Refugee children almost inevitably display feelings of panic and terror. In later stages they may entertain elaborate fantasies of retaliating against those who have wronged them and their parents. They may also feel resentment toward their parents for "throwing them" into such chaos.[19]

Another theme found among asylum seekers is a profound wish to return home "as soon as things calm down." Gustavo Perez-Firmat, who came to the United States as a child of Cuban refugees, describes beautifully the ethos of middle-class Cuban refugees in Miami. He reports how during their first months in the United States, many Cuban refugee families lived out of suitcases, refusing to unpack because of a wishful certainty that "any day now" Castro would fall and they could return to their beloved island. Over the years, they did unpack their suitcases, but at Christmas their toast became "Next Year [we'll be] in Cuba."

The factors that matter in the experience of refugee children overlap considerably with what matters in the lives of other immigrant children. The physical and psychological availability of parents, the family's socioeconomic background, and the context in which the family resettles all shape the transition for both refugee and immigrant children. But the trauma suffered by refugee children before departing their homeland greatly influences their subsequent adaptations.

Research suggests a series of complex and sometimes contradictory social outcomes in the new country. Some children who arrived with earlier waves of Southeast Asian refugees, as well as with more recent waves of Central American asylum seekers, tend to overachieve, going on to four-year colleges in disproportionately high numbers.[20] Conversely, many of them tend to underachieve, dropping out of school and joining gangs in alarming numbers.[21] Most fall between these two extremes, and certain patterns characterize each group. Among those who drop out of school and join gangs, alienation from the family, lack of social cohesion in the community, and lack of meaningful opportunities coalesce in disconcerting ways. Those who succeed "against all odds," by contrast, seem to come from more cohesive families and are often motivated by a wish to give back to their parents, to make their sacrifices and suffering worthwhile.[22]

Transnational Pathways

For many, perhaps most, immigration represents a permanent move. In such cases children are raised to become competent members of the new society—a complex task that perhaps defines the most important challenge to the immigrant family. For others, immigration is a temporary state before eventually returning "home."

"Success" for many immigrants in the past and present has meant exactly the opposite of what most nonimmigrant members of the mainstream culture would define as a successful immigrant journey. For some types of immigrants, success is *not* assimilating and growing deep roots in a new land. Rather "success" is returning home after achieving the goals that motivated them to migrate in the first place: earning the resources (financial and social) that would enable them to have a better life *back home*.[23]

Two distinct patterns of immigration have been associated with this strategy. The first is that of the "target earner" who sets out to a new land in search of better-paying work with the intention of returning home permanently when the earnings goal has been reached. In this case, one or both parents migrate for a few months (or a few years) while children remain in the country of origin with other relatives.

Sojourners, the second type, move periodically to and from, and sometimes within, the new country, often following a seasonal cycle. Mexican migrant workers have for decades embodied this experience. The work they tend to do is typically extremely hard and poorly paid, and native workers are simply not interested in doing it. A farmer with experience in hiring workers for such jobs said of his attempts to hire nonimmigrant, local workers: "Four young people came in for the jobs. Two quit before lunch, and the other two finished out the day but they never came back."[24] Sometimes sojourners are part of former "guest worker" programs, such as the "bracero" program that brought large numbers of Mexican agricultural workers to California. These workers are often referred to simply as migrant workers.[25]

The experiences of the children of sojourners in rural areas are quite different from those of immigrants who permanently settle in urban centers. Children of seasonal migrants face several challenges. Those who move with their parents following the crop cycle experience frequent interruptions in their schooling, and find it difficult to synchronize a school plan among various districts (within a given state, across states, and internationally). Some face pressure to prematurely join their parents in the field to earn money that will help the family survive.[26]

It should be noted that not all sojourners are agricultural workers. In recent years, Eastern European housepainters and construction workers have typically arrived in the Northeast during the spring and summer to pursue their trade. Typically, however, they are not accompanied by children.

Yet another type of temporary immigrant—binationals—continually shuttles between "here" (the new country) and "there" (the old country). This new pattern is said to define the lives of growing numbers of immigrants.

In recent years, a number of scholars of immigration have argued that new transnational and global forces structure the journeys of immigrants in more complex ways than previously seen.[27] This research suggests that many immigrants are players—economically, politically, and culturally—both in their newly adopted lands *and* in their communities of origin.[28] These new transnational pathways suggest important questions about the lives of immigrant children. But very little solid data exists on how this emerging transnationalism may be patterning these children's experiences. In our own research, teachers and administrators disapprovingly reported to us that some immigrant students periodically "disappear," especially around holidays, and return weeks later, by which time they have fallen behind in their schoolwork.

While some children do indeed go back and forth, we have found that the claims that immigrant children today are deeply engaged in "transnational shuttling" are inflated. Indeed, as we report in the next chapter, children of immigrants display fewer transnational behaviors and attitudes than many might have predicted.

For many immigrant children, especially those from modest backgrounds, it is simply prohibitively expensive to travel back and forth. Transnational shuttling seems to be determined largely by three key factors: parental financial resources, legal status, and proximity to the country of origin. Those who are poor and without documentation, and who live far from the country of origin, are indeed least likely to engage in transnational shuttling.

Undocumented Status

Social scientists interested in immigration agree that actions—and inactions—of governments influence migratory processes. States are in the business of regulating the movement of people—both internally and internationally. The right to leave a country (that is, the right to emigrate) is a relatively recent phenomenon.[29]

Nation-states regulate, and carefully police, the inflow of international immigrants. They also generate policies designed to establish who is a "legal" or "illegal" immigrant, who is an "asylum seeker," a "refugee," or a "temporary guest worker." States regulate how many immigrants are legally admitted every year. Since 1990, for example, an average of about a million legal immigrants have been allowed into the United States annually. Yet legal immigration into Northwestern Europe was greatly curbed following the oil crisis of the early 1970s.[30]

While the state wields substantial power over international migration, it is nearly powerless to control "illegal" or undocumented immigration. In many parts of the world, undocumented immigration periodically emerges as a theme for unsettling political debate. This enduring problem suggests that immigration is now structured by powerful economic and social forces and cultural practices that seem impervious to state actions such as controls of international borders.[31]

In the United States, estimates suggest that two to five million undocumented immigrants make up roughly 10 percent of the total foreign-born (immigrant) population.[32] The best estimates suggest that every year, 250,000 to 500,000 undocumented immigrants enter the United States.

Public perception about the issue of visa overstayers is minimal since many in the United States see "illegal" immigration as a problem only at the border of Mexico and the United States. But only about half of today's undocumented immigrants to the United States pass through our southern border without inspection or documentation. The other half are visa overstayers—people who typically fly into international airports with proper documentation and simply overstay their permits. This is a highly heterogeneous group of people that includes professionals, skilled and unskilled workers, tourists, and students from all parts of the world. Many may find it surprising that Canadians are the fourth largest group of undocumented immigrants to the United States today.

It is important to stress that the majority of the children of immigrants are documented. Yet some are not. While absolute numbers are impossible to obtain, it is reasonable to assume that 10 to 15 percent of foreign-born children in the United States are undocumented.[33] In California, for example, 200,000 to 400,000 undocumented children are estimated to be enrolled in schools.

Many of these children come to the United States accompanied by a migrant adult, but their crossings can be quite complex. For example, recent data reveal a surprising pattern. According to a Human Rights Watch report,

> Each year thousands of children enter the United States illegally. Some of the children come with parents or relatives, but most come alone; some are refugees fleeing persecution in their home countries, while others hope to find work and send money home to their poverty-stricken families.
>
> When they reach the United States (usually with little money and no ability to speak or understand English), these children face an uncertain future. Some manage to reach migrant labor communities or to find relatives already living in American cities, and they merge unnoticed into the American population, often becoming legal permanent residents in time. But many of these children are apprehended by the Immigration and Naturalization Service (INS), which in 1990

arrested 8,500 undocumented children, 70 percent of whom were unaccompanied by an adult guardian.[34]

Unaccompanied children who are "too young to be released on
their own recognizance" and those who have no relatives in the
United States are placed in detention by the INS.[35] Indeed, thousands of undocumented children are kept for extended periods in
prisons alongside adult convicts. Although this number represents
only a small proportion of undocumented children in American society, Human Rights Watch found that these children receive no education, no legal or psychological services, and little or no access to
recreational facilities.

The legal status of an immigrant child influences—perhaps more
so than the national origins and socioeconomic background of the
parents—his or her experiences and life chances. Immigration is
stressful for all children, as we elaborate in Chapter 3. For children
and families who are undocumented, the stresses and complications
run very deep.

While documented immigrant children are often excited and feel
a sense of adventure about coming to the United States, undocumented children find the journey always stressful and sometimes
traumatic. Since the intensification of INS efforts to curtail illegal
immigration, initiated in the mid-1990s, deaths, rapes, and acci-
dents at the border have increased.[36]

After managing the dangerous border crossing, undocumented
parents inevitably remain vulnerable to the threat of deportation.
They also are subject to exploitation by unscrupulous employers
who take advantage of their vulnerability. Reports of undocumented
workers living and working in inhumane conditions are common-
place. Thai women working in the Los Angeles garment district were
found literally chained to their workstations for long hours. Some
Chinese workers who had incurred debts of thousands of dollars to
come to the United States were kept in indentured servitude for
years by the smugglers who brought them. Another notorious case
involved deaf-mute Mexicans in New York living and working in
what were characterized as "slavery-like" conditions.[37]

On a less dramatic level, undocumented parents remain vulnerable to threats of deportation from employers who may not want to pay them, envious coworkers, and suspicious neighbors. There have also been reports that documented husbands use threats of deportation as a means to control their undocumented wives.[38]

Many undocumented children report that they feel constantly "hunted." The parents may severely constrict their activities outside the home for fear that they will be apprehended. It is frightening to anticipate that their children may be detained at any time. For children with undocumented parents, there is also the fear that the parent will be caught and deported. A common terror many undocumented children experience is that they will never be reunited with their parent.

Many undocumented children and their parents feel that anyone they encounter, especially those in official positions such as police officers, teachers, and nurses, may turn them in to the INS. After California's controversial Proposition 187 passed—the law that would have denied publicly funded schooling and health services to undocumented immigrants—there were widespread reports that those in official positions were not to be trusted.[39]

In such contexts of distrust, undocumented children may remain guarded with their teachers, doctors, and nurses. During our research, we found for example that some undocumented families did not write accurate phone numbers or addresses on parent contact forms at schools for fear that the information would be given to INS agents. This made it impossible for school nurses to get in touch with parents in an emergency.

One of the most demoralizing aspects of undocumented status is its effect on the educational aspirations of immigrant children. Most immigrant children (including those without legal documentation) enter their new society with high hopes for becoming well educated. During the first year of our study, 97 percent of our participants believed that education was critical to their future in the new country. Many completed a sentence that began "In life the most important thing is . . . " with "school" or "education."

Highly motivated and school-oriented undocumented students

are shattered to realize that their legal status will prevent them from pursuing their dream of a college education. Recently, one such case in Texas gained notoriety. One of the most gifted musicians in a competitive high school had been accepted into several prestigious Ivy League colleges. Though he had been in the United States since preschool age, he found that he would not be able to go onto college because he was an undocumented immigrant.[40]

We have come across many such devastating cases over the years in our research and work with immigrant children.[41] The bottom line is that undocumented students can not enter the postsecondary system or obtain any form of financial aid without proper INS documentation.

We found that older children feel a terrible sense of injustice when they first discover that they cannot go beyond high school: a feeling of anger is followed by a sense of hopelessness and depression. Many simply give up on schooling in their last year of high school. In some cases, high school students do not know that they are undocumented until they begin to think about college and their parents are forced to tell them.

Special issues arise in families that have a mix of documented and undocumented children–a rather common occurrence. In such families, unique dynamics tend to develop. In some cases, the undocumented child may unconsciously become the family's scapegoat while the documented child may occupy the role of "the golden child." This imbalance creates tensions and resentments, as well as guilt and shame.

Undocumented immigrant children have been a part of the past, are a part of the present, and will be a part of the future of U.S. immigration. Indeed, the vast majority of these children will remain in the United States, and many of them will eventually become citizens. It is therefore important that such children be given full access to schooling and health services. While some have worried about the costs incurred by taxpayers in educating undocumented immigrant children, in the long term the costs of *not* educating them are even greater.

2

RETHINKING IMMIGRATION

The Haitian toddler who floats to shore with her father, the son of a Chinese worker who overstays her visa, and the Canadian adolescent with a green card in hand travel very different pathways into the United States. But they all will be transformed by the immigrant experience.

A significant factor shaping the children's experience is what we term the "ethos of reception." This includes not only the opportunities available but also, just as importantly, the general social and cultural climate they encounter. This climate is largely shaped by the general attitudes and beliefs held by members of the new society about immigration and immigrants. These attitudes trickle down to the children and affect their perceptions, developing identities, and behaviors.

The Ambivalence of the Native-Born

Immigration is at the core of both the history and the destiny of the United States. The United States was founded on the travails of immigrants; over the centuries, it has experienced steady streams as well as massive waves of immigrants who have continued to transform the landscape. As a result, the immigrant experience has generated cultural narratives of mythical proportions. At the root of the debate about immigration lie two very different views of immigrants. At one extreme is a benign and idealized view of immigrants, and at the other, a vilified caricature.

Stories that idealize immigration help us create the values that make up our cultural core. Perhaps the most classic version of this shared narrative goes something like this: Poor hardworking European peasants, with great ingenuity and hard work, gladly give up their counterproductive Old World ways (including language, customs, and values) to become prosperous, proud, and loyal Americans.[1]

In this familiar narrative, immigrants enact a reassuring script that recycles the myth of the American project. According to the founding myth of the nation, the United States is unique because it took in millions of humble foreigners and made them into successful and loyal Americans. Immigrant "courage, creativity, determination" embodies the energy of a proud America.[2] As Barbara Jordan, former chair of the Commission on Immigration Reform, put it, immigrants "remind ourselves of . . . what makes us American."[3]

These scripts have carefully defined roles for the new immigrants. They require, as a grand finale, that immigrants become just like us. True differences must be erased, and cultural diversity must only be celebrated in superficial, "folkloristic" forms. The terms of the bargain are clear: to become proud and loyal Americans, immigrants must first "give up" all meaningful cultural and linguistic differences. When immigrants resist this script, anxieties are unleashed— and resounding cries of the "disuniting of America!" "Balkanization of California!" or "tearing of the American fabric!" are voiced in the public imaginary.

At the opposite end of the narrative spectrum is a somewhat sinister and uncanny view of immigrants. In these scripts, immigration articulates and unleashes powerful anxieties about "losing control" of our society, our language, and our economy. A 1993 *New York Times* survey indicated that nearly 50 percent of all respondents believed that new immigrants are "taking jobs from citizens."[4]

Large-scale immigration engenders the fear that we are "inundated, swamped, submerged, engulfed, awash" by new arrivals. Ruth Coffey, the head of Stop Immigration Now (SIN) stated, "I have no intention of being the object of 'conquest,' peaceful or otherwise, by Latinos, Asians, Blacks, Arabs or any other group of individuals who have claimed my country."[5]

Anti-immigration narratives typically deploy images of chaos in which growing waves of "aliens" threaten our way of life. In the words of a border resident in San Diego, California—words that sum up the worst fears of many—the country is "under siege": "You find the huge gangs of illegal aliens that line our streets, shake down our schoolchildren, spread diseases like malaria, and roam our neighborhoods looking for work or homes to rob. We are under siege . . . and we have been deserted by those whose job it is to protect us from this flood of illegal aliens."[6]

In recent years, the dominant anti-immigration narrative has ignited fears that immigrants are flooding our shores, taking our jobs, overwhelming our social services, and inflating our crime rate. Furthermore, immigrants are seen by many as coming from backward cultures and ethnic backgrounds that make it impossible for them to assimilate into mainstream American society.[7] Are these views remarkably different from those held about past waves of immigrants?

Historical Themes

The historical record strongly suggests that in other eras Americans have greeted immigrants in nearly the same way. Historian Rita Simon conducted an exhaustive review of media representations of immigrants in the United States over one hundred years (1880 to 1980) and examined fifty years of public opinion polls from their beginnings in the late 1930s.[8] Her findings illustrate a classic pattern of response to new arrivals—American citizens have held consistently negative attitudes toward people wishing to enter the United States, and the more recent the immigrant group, the more negative the opinion.[9] On the whole, while the people who came in earlier waves are thought to have been "good folk," new immigrants are viewed by many as "pure scum."[10]

In 1920, an essayist in one of the two largest periodicals of the time, the *North American Review,* wrote about the immigrants of his era: "They come in far greater numbers, vermin infested, alien in languages and in spirit, with racial imprints which can be neither burned out nor bred out, packs on their back, leading little children by the hand. And like the hordes of old, they are destined to conquer us in the end, unless by some miracle of human controversy we conquer them first." Around the same time, a sociologist observed: "The United States seems fated never to be free from trouble attendant to race and immigration. First it was the 'Negroes,' then it was the Chinese and the Japanese, now it is the Mexicans." The pseudoscience of eugenics of the early decades of this century gave deep anti-immigrant sentiment a cloak of rationality. But whereas in earlier times concern was over postulated biological and racial inferiority, in more recent times, as we discuss later, we are witnessing the use of so-called cultural differences as the banner of those who are against immigration. Then, as now, crime was linked to the "mass of degraded, lawless, and mentally defective aliens who have gained admission or who have come in illegally . . . Is not the enormous expense of maintaining asylums, institutions, hospitals, prisons, penitentiaries, and the like due in considerable measure to the foreign born, socially inadequate aliens?"[11]

During the 1920s a frequent contributor to the *Saturday Evening Post* contrasted the "old immigrants" (from Northern Europe) with the "new immigrants" (those from Southern and Eastern Europe). Old immigrants, he claimed, were able to blend into the melting pot. But new immigrants, he asserted, were entering the country simply to make money by any means before returning to their homelands. Maintaining that many were illiterate, he argued that they would be difficult to assimilate: "If the United States is the melting pot, something is wrong with the heating system, for an inconveniently large portion of the new immigration floats around in unsightly indigestible lumps. Of recent years, the contents of the melting pot have stood badly in need of straining in order that the refuse might be removed and deposited in the customary receptacle for such things." The fear was that "America has largely become the dumping ground for the world's human riffraff, who couldn't make a living in their own countries."[12] The immigrants of the time were viewed as intellectually inferior, lazy, crime-prone, and altogether unassimilable.

The historical record clearly shows that immigration has generated powerful and enduring anxieties. Attitudes toward immigrants seem to become more positive mostly in retrospect. With the safe distance of time, we tend to celebrate the past achievements of various immigrant groups. On the other hand, new immigrants are nearly always viewed with considerable suspicion. Many fear them as competitors at best or sinister aliens at worst.

Responses to the New Immigration

In recent years, fears about immigration have led to several anti-immigrant initiatives. In 1994, California voters overwhelmingly approved Proposition 187, known as the "Save our State" initiative, claiming:

> [The People of California] have suffered and are suffering economic hardship caused by the presence of illegal aliens in this state.
>
> That they have suffered and are suffering personal injury and damage caused by the criminal conduct of illegal aliens in this state.
>
> That they have a right to the protection of their government from any person or persons entering this country unlawfully.
>
> Therefore, the people of California declare their intention to provide for cooperation between their agencies of state and local government with the federal government, and to establish a system of required notification by and between such agencies to prevent illegal aliens in the United States from receiving benefits or public services in the State of California.[13]

Currently, the law is not being fully implemented. If it were, some 300,000 to 400,000 undocumented immigrant children in California would be banned from enrolling in public schools.[14]

Public anxieties over immigration—especially illegal immigration—have inspired a host of other legislative and policy initiatives. These policies were designed to bar immigrants from receiving a variety of publicly funded services. More stringent border controls also sought to deter further undocumented immigration.[15]

There is a tendency to view immigration as a uniquely American experience. But many postindustrial democracies such as Germany, France, and Japan have been facing similar concerns.[16] How have these countries responded to immigration? Are their concerns significantly different from those found in the United States? To para-

phrase Tolstoy, when it comes to immigration, nearly all of the families of the postindustrial world seem to be unhappy in the same way.
Policies to contain the "immigration problem" have also flourished
in Europe because many believe that (1) there are too many immigrants, (2) they are threatening the economic well-being of the continent, (3) they add to the crime problem, and (4) they are transforming cities in ways that many find culturally disorienting and
personally unsettling.[17]

Recurring Concerns about Immigration

In the United States, immigration continues to generate debate and
controversy. Underlying these debates are some strong assumptions
about immigration. But are the assumptions correct? Which are
florid exaggerations and where are the grains of truth? What are the
realties about immigration?

IMMIGRANTS AND THE ECONOMY

The economy is nearly always a key factor in determining perceptions and attitudes toward immigrants. A team of Princeton University sociologists conducted a series of comprehensive studies of
American public opinion polls on immigration.[18] In a study of national surveys by twenty different organizations over a thirty-year
period, they found that, historically, a very strong correlation exists
between anti-immigrant sentiment and economic anxiety, particularly around unemployment rates. Put simply, when unemployment
rates are high, anti-immigrant feelings are also usually high. Likewise, when unemployment rates drop and there is optimism about
the economy, anti-immigration sentiment fades.

This and other studies suggest that immigration is an enduring
concern lurking just below the surface of public consciousness in the
United States. In times of economic prosperity, immigration is either ignored or superficially celebrated. In times of economic uncer-
tainty, immigration once again surfaces as a cause for concern.

Many studies on immigration and the economy attempt to evaluate the overarching fiscal implications of large-scale immigration.
Some explore whether immigrants produce a net gain or a net loss

in terms of tax revenues they generate versus the publicly funded services they require (such as education, health, and the criminal justice system). Other studies examine broader economic features of immigration such as whether immigrants stimulate or stagnate the economy. Still others consider the issues of competition between native workers and immigrant workers and the new skills that immigrants bring with them.

Studies of immigration's economic effects reveal a complex picture. Some claim that the new immigrants are an overall burden to the U.S. economy, while others suggest in equally strong terms that immigrants continue to be an important asset to it.[19]

Those who see immigration as a burden maintain that new immigrants (particularly those with little education and few skills) quickly become dependent on the entitlements of the welfare state.[20] This school of thought holds that the new immigrants end up "costing" more in terms of publicly funded services than they contribute in taxes.[21] Those who see the new immigrants as contributors to the economy seem to speak another language altogether. They argue that the new arrivals—documented and undocumented—contribute far more to the economy than they use in services.[22]

Other researchers have attempted to study the economic consequences of immigration in broader terms. Some have claimed that new immigrants play a critical role in stimulating and reinvigorating "abandoned" urban zones by opening ethnic businesses, and that through the so-called multiplier effect they have created job opportunities for the native born.[23] Native-born women, too, may have benefited from large-scale immigration because affordable childcare by foreign workers has helped many participate in the formal labor market.[24] Still others argue that immigrant workers will be increasingly critical when large numbers of baby boomers begin to retire en masse and become "consumers" of social security and Medicare.[25]

A poll of eminent economists, which included members of the President's Council of Economic Advisors and former presidents of the American Economic Association, reveals some interesting findings. These economists overwhelmingly viewed immigration in positive economic terms. When asked "On balance, what effect has twentieth-century immigration had on the nation's economic growth?" 81 percent responded "very favorably" and 19 percent responded "slightly favorably." When asked "What level of immigration would have the most favorable impact on the U.S. standard of living?" fully 63 percent of the economists responded that more immigration would have a favorable effect. (Note that none of them thought that fewer immigrants would have the most favorable effect on the U.S. economy.) Did these economists feel that recent immigrants are "qualitatively different in economic terms than immigrants in past years?" The vast majority (76 percent) responded that recent immigrants have had "about the same impact" on the U.S. economy than past waves of immigrants. Even when considering the highly charged question, "What impact does *illegal* immigration in its current magnitude have on the U.S. economy?" 74 percent indicated that illegal immigrants have a positive effect. Although this survey has some obvious limitations (for example, it is not at all clear whether these economists are basing their opinions on their own research on the economics of immigration), it does reveal that leading American economists seem to have a positive opinion of the economic implications of immigration.

A recent study by the National Research Council (NRC) on the economic, demographic, and fiscal effects of the new immigration suggests that "immigration produces net economic gains for domestic residents." The NRC study calculates that the immigration-related "domestic gain may run on the order of $1 billion to $10 billion a year."[26] Although the NRC reports overall positive implications of immigration on the U.S. economy, it does present a number of caveats. For example, the NRC data suggest that "immigrants receive more in services than they pay in taxes." They imply that there are

three main reasons why immigrants receive more in services than they pay in taxes: (1) immigrant-headed households include more school-aged children than native households on average, and therefore currently consume more educational services; (2) immigrant-headed households are poorer than native households on average, and therefore receive more state and locally funded income transfers; and (3) immigrant-headed households have lower incomes and own less property than native households on average, and thus pay lower state and local taxes.[27]

Some scholars of immigration argue that the disparity in the allocation of tax revenue generated by immigrants between the state and the federal levels is another source of anxiety about the economics of immigration. A prominent political scientist at the University of California observed that "California suffers from an unfair distribution of the tax revenues contributed by immigrants themselves, with the Federal government keeping the lion's share and returning to heavily impacted states and localities considerably less than is needed to provide basic human services to the immigrants they are absorbing." This inherent discrepancy between local and federal interests was behind the unsuccessful lawsuit filed by California against the federal government for the funds needed to provide services to immigrants and their families.[28]

Other studies have specifically examined the issue of the competition for jobs between immigrants and native workers. Charges have been made that immigrants take away jobs from native workers and that they tend to "depress" the wages of nonimmigrant workers. The National Research Council addressed this issue and concluded that large-scale immigration has contributed to a modest drop in the minimum wage only for the *lowest skilled* native workers (a 5 percent drop in wages since 1980 among high school dropouts).[29] The NRC concluded that immigrants do not, on aggregate, depress the wages of most nonimmigrant workers.[30]

What about the claim that immigrants take away jobs from non-immigrant citizens? Several immigration researchers have pointed out that this assumption is simply not true.[31] In fact, in the words of the head of the Carnegie Endowment's Immigration Policy Program, "the overall impact of immigrant workers on U.S. workers is small."[32]

The question has also been raised whether immigrants may be competing for jobs at the low end of the spectrum with African

Americans, edging them out of work and deflating wages.[33] The National Research Council is unequivocal on this point: "While some have suspected that blacks suffer disproportionately from the inflow of low-skilled immigrants, none of the available evidence suggests that they have been particularly hard-hit on a national level. Some have lost their jobs, especially in places where immigrants are concentrated. But the majority of blacks live elsewhere, and their economic fortunes are tied to other factors."[34]

To conclude, while the debate rages on (especially about the role of low-skilled immigrants), the preponderance of evidence from the most reliable sources points to a relative economic benefit at the national level and modest economic costs at the local level.[35]

IMMIGRATION AND THE WELFARE STATE

In recent years, it has been claimed that the post-1965 wave of immigration has gathered momentum because of incentives provided by the welfare state. Many believe that immigrants come to take advantage of publicly funded services such as Medicaid, food stamps, and education. Former California governor Pete Wilson repeatedly claimed that the new immigrants were "drawn by the giant magnet of Federal incentives."[36] Media stories of pregnant immigrant women crossing the border to give birth in a U.S. hospital (free of charge) fuel resentment among many who view immigrants as freeloaders.[37] Another charge, also widely reported in the print media, relates to elderly immigrants coming late in life to the United States to take advantage of many costly services provided to the elderly in this country. From birth to death, many worry that immigrants take advantage of the system.

Because Medicare is one of the most expensive transfer payments made by the government (along with Social Security) there has been a great deal of concern about the costs of delivering health care to a large population of new arrivals. What do the most reliable research findings suggest? An overview of the specific issue of health care and undocumented immigrants finds extremely inflated cost estimates circulating in the press.[38] More broadly, researchers in the health sciences have found that immigrants (including those from poorer countries) tend to be healthier than individuals born in the United States.[39] They have identified an epidemiological paradox known as the healthy immigrant effect. Immigrants tend to be healthier, have lower infant mortality and morbidity rates, and therefore are less likely than native-born Americans to seek out publicly funded health services.[40]

A team of prominent UCLA researchers conducted several studies on access to health care among immigrants and their children. Using data based on two separate surveys, they considered immigrant use of physician services.[41] They found that one-quarter of all immigrant children do not have a regular source of care; more than a third of Latino children have no usual source of care; and fully one-third of all immigrant children reported no physician visits within the past year.[42]

Certainly some immigrants, including undocumented immigrants, use the public health care system, particularly emergency room services. It is also true that there have been a number of scandalous cases in which immigrants of high status fraudulently used publicly funded health treatment in the United States.[43] But research suggests that immigrants and the children of immigrants tend to underutilize the health care system.[44] Ironically, immigrants probably pay more into the health system than they take out of it.

Immigrants tend to receive fewer social benefits than nonimmigrant citizens, though some studies suggest that the elderly and some groups of refugees are more likely to be dependent on publicly funded benefits for their survival.[45] The concept that immigrants may end up abusing the welfare system is justifiably upsetting to many. The notion articulated by some that immigrants come to the United States *because* of welfare is, however, unfounded. Once in the United States immigrants, like the rest of us, attempt to maximize their self-interest and take full advantage of all opportunities available. The fact that upon their arrival the new immigrants encounter the structures of a (albeit shrinking) welfare state, and use the resources available to them, is very different from the charge that immigrants are *motivated* to come to parasitically plug into the welfare system.

The valuable immigrant workers—those on whom many businesses have come to rely—have families and children who need services. It is unrealistic to desire immigrant workers *without* being willing to absorb the costs of having them come with their families.

ILLEGAL IMMIGRATION

A team of Princeton researchers recently reported that nearly 70 percent of respondents in a national public opinion survey thought that *most* immigrants in the United States were here illegally.[46] In fact, the majority of immigrants in the United States are legal immigrants. As noted in Chapter 1, there are 2.5 million to 5 million undocumented ("illegal") immigrants currently residing in the United States. Although this is a significant figure, it represents only about 10 to 15 percent of the total foreign-born population. Further, many of these undocumented immigrants have family members who are U.S. citizens or permanent legal residents.[47]

Although approximately half of all undocumented immigration takes place at international airports, the public believes that the vast majority of undocumented immigrants come across the southern border of the United States. In response, in 1997 Congress doubled the budget of the INS to a total of 3.1 billion dollars. At the end of the century, there were nearly 7,000 border patrol agents and Congress has mandated that the border control force reach a total of 10,000 agents.

These border control initiatives generate an image of state control and reinforce the erroneous claim that the solution to the problem of illegal immigration is to be found on the border. But illegal entry into the United States can only superficially be managed at the border. An intelligent and productive policy to contain the levels of illegal immigration will doubtlessly require an ambitious program of international cooperation to deal with the extremely complex economic, social, and cultural determinants of immigration.

IMMIGRATION AND CRIME

Adding to the problem of Americans' misperceptions about how many illegal immigrants there are is the short semantic leap from "illegal alien" to "criminal alien." A nationwide poll found that 59 percent of those surveyed agreed with the statement "immigrants add to the crime problem."[48]

Many fear criminal activities associated with immigration. In the words of a former INS director in San Diego, California, "a torrent of people [are] flooding here, bringing all kinds of criminal elements and terrorists."[49] Others worry about the "new criminals . . . undocumented aliens from Mexico, some of whom live here but many of whom sleep in their native land and cross daily into the United States to commit their crimes."[50] Still others have become concerned that immigrants in the United States working with or for foreign terrorist groups will bring their causes to American shores. As festivities for millennium celebrations were being planned in New York, Seattle, and elsewhere, there was great anxiety when an Algerian citizen (said to be a member of a terrorist cell) was apprehended while crossing the U.S.-Canadian border allegedly carrying explosives.[51]

Gordon Allport, in his classic psychological study of prejudice, argues that all irrational fears are deformed elaborations based on some kernel of truth.[52] Nearly a quarter of all inmates in federal custody today are foreign-born, an alarming statistic that periodically fuels the anti-immigration fires. Let us examine the complexities behind these figures.

It should be noted that "foreign-born" does not necessarily mean "immigrant." Many of the foreign-born involved in criminal activity cannot be considered immigrants in the traditional sense of the word. Many foreign-born criminals held in federal custody are notorious lords of Latin American drug cartels and "foot soldiers" of the booming drug trade between Latin America, the Caribbean, and the United States, who have no intention of staying in the United States. In addition, many of those who show up in the foreign-born statistics are "border bandits" (also called the "rob and return bunch") who work with some impunity on both sides of the U.S.-Mexican border.[53]

Many of the foreign-born criminals are in the business of smuggling undocumented workers. Tougher immigration controls at the southern border have paradoxically led to a great deal of illegal activity, including more sophisticated smuggling operations and an expanding document-counterfeiting industry.[54] In particular, only approximately 10 to 12 percent of those arrested in areas with heavy immigrant populations are undocumented immigrants. In a study of San Diego Country, California (with a large undocumented immigrant population), there exists "substantial unanimity among police that, as a group, migrant workers do not appear to be responsible for much serious crime . . . they tend to be arrested for 'public order misdemeanors,' such as urinating in public, and nonviolent 'survival crimes,' such as thefts of bedding, food, and cash." Furthermore, migrant workers are more likely than nonmigrant U.S. citizens to be the victims of border bandit crime.[55]

There are few reliable studies on crime among immigrants as defined in this book (that is, those moving across international borders with the intention to permanently settle here).[56] After reviewing the limited number of studies on the subject, however, a noted immigration scholar concluded that "the rate of all crime has been less among immigrants than among natives."[57] On the whole, those opposed to immigration have distorted the prevalence of immigrant (as distinguished from "foreign-born") crime.[58]

Yet even if immigrants are unfairly perceived to commit more crimes than they do, the marginalization of large numbers of immigrants spells significant danger for the future. If large numbers of immigrant children are not educated and graduate or are pushed out of schools without the required tools to make a living, it should not be surprising if crime and delinquency become serious issues as these children enter adolescence and adulthood.[59]

CHILDREN OF IMMIGRANTS WILL NOT ASSIMILATE

The concerns that immigrant children "can not" or "will not" assimilate to mainstream American culture are two sides of a single coin that are invoked sometimes separately and sometimes concurrently. The idea that the children of immigrants *cannot* be assimilated is based partly on the assumption that the "quality" of today's immigrants is somehow below the quality of immigrants from previous eras.[60] While "old immigrants" are celebrated, new immigrants are seen as falling short.

In his book *Alien Nation,* journalist Peter Brimelow articulates the fears of many: "The latest immigrants are different from those who came before. These newcomers are less educated, less skilled, more prone to be in trouble with the law, less inclined to share American culture and values, and altogether less inclined to become American in name and spirit."[61]

Brimelow captures at once both very old and more recent anti-immigrant sensibilities.[62] His claim that immigrants are "less inclined" to embrace their new country is part of a larger critique of the new immigration in this era of transnationalism and multiculturalism. Accounts of culturally dissonant practices such as arranged marriages involving young girls or female genital mutilations continually horrify Americans. Many were alarmed when on the eve of the vote for California's Proposition 187, Latino youngsters (some proudly displaying Mexican flags) took to the streets of San Francisco, Los Angeles, and San Diego to protest the initiative. The flag incident was interpreted by some as symptomatic of a studied refusal to "assimilate."[63]

Anxieties about the loyalties and cultural integration of new immigrants circulate with similar force in other countries, such as Belgium, Austria, and France. In Parisian schools, a debate exploded about the meanings of veils worn by some North African immigrant students. Did it mean that the girls and their families were rejecting French secular culture in favor of an enduring loyalty to North Africa? Why did they not want to become French?[64]

Many fear that new transnational impulses subvert the "assimilation" of immigrant children into their new country. Using a lowest-common-denominator definition, "assimilation" is used as shorthand for learning English, getting a good job, and settling down. The subtext we hear in conversations with teachers, principals, and others working with immigrant children tends to be monothematic: My grandparents came here dirt-poor from Europe, they struggled to learn English, worked hard, and assimilated—why can't the new immigrants do the same? Why can't they learn English and become American? Why can't they settle down, give up their culture, and become like the rest of us?

This perception of history is incomplete on many levels. Earlier European immigration was divided into distinct, time-limited waves, so it was easier to assess a group's journey into the American mainstream. While the foreign-born generation made modest gains, much more was expected of subsequent generations in terms of linguistic facility and socioeconomic mobility. Parity with the mainstream was expected within a few generations. By then, immigrants were said to have culturally "disappeared"; whatever ethnic distinctions remained were thought to be purely symbolic.[65] With Anglicized names and no distinctive accent, the children and grandchildren of White European immigrants became the raw material that went into the making of the "melting pot" ideology.

Among new immigrants, however, another pattern is unfolding. The vast majority of the new immigrants are people of color, so they and their children cannot disappear into white mainstream America. Another distinctive feature of the new immigration is that among such groups as the Mexican-origin population, there is a constant replenishment through more or less uninterrupted immigration flows. Among Mexican immigrants today "the presence in the same neighborhoods (and indeed, often in the same households) of virtually any combination of U.S.-born Mexican Americans, permanent immigrants (both officially sanctioned and undocumented), long-term and short-term sojourners, and the U.S.-born and foreign-born children of all these groups" complicates efforts to examine patterns of assimilation over time.[66]

It is important not to confound the experiences and adaptations of third- or fourth-generation Mexican Americans with those of more recent arrivals. In the case of populations that are continually renewed by ongoing immigration, a great deal of assimilation occurs behind the scenes.[67] But for an observer who is outside looking in, it may be hard to differentiate between recent arrivals and long-term residents. From this vantage point, it may indeed look like "they" are not assimilating and not learning English.

The debate over English as the official language of the United States is inspired in large part by cultural anxiety about the new immigrants' imagined refusal to learn the language. This view is behind the English-only movement, which produced the following statement: "When linguistic unity has broken down, our energies and resources flow into tensions, hostilities, prejudices, and resentments. These develop and persist. Within a few years, if the breakdown persists, there will be no retreat. It becomes irrevocable, irreversible. Society as we know it can fade into noisy Babel and chaos."[68]

The data on language attitudes and language behaviors among new immigrants, however, prove that immigrants care deeply about learning English.[69] A study based on 1990 census data found that over three-quarters of all immigrants reported that they spoke English fluently after being in the country for ten years.[70] In fact, even in areas where there is a high density of new immigrants, knowledge of English among the children of immigrants is "nearly universal."[71]

We asked the immigrant children in our sample whether they thought learning English is important. The overwhelming majority—99 percent—responded with a resounding yes. While 47 percent of these children admitted that learning English is hard, 92 percent also reported that they liked learning the new language. Valuing English, however, did not mean abandoning one's language of origin: 90 percent of the children indicated that maintaining their first language was also important to them.[72]

As has been true for previous groups of immigrants, the longer the children are here the more likely they are to distance themselves linguistically from their parents and eventually lose their native language.[73] It is quite possible for a first-generation Spanish-speaking immigrant who moves into a predominantly Spanish-speaking neighborhood and who works among and for Spanish-speaking people to never learn to speak anything more than the most rudimentary English. It would be highly unusual, however, for her children or grandchildren to not be predominantly English speakers. English rapidly becomes the dominant language for the vast majority of the children of immigrants.[74]

Even so, the massive concentration of highly visible immigrants in a handful of urban centers, such as the greater Los Angeles basin, Miami, and certain neighborhoods in New York and Chicago, has produced extremely complex cultural formations and transformed the cities.[75] In those areas, there has been a verifiable explosion of Spanish-speaking print media, television, and radio markets. This infrastructure makes it easy for some immigrants to maintain their cultural models and linguistic practices. These cultural dynamics are not only highly visible and audible but also upsetting to many monolingual English-speaking residents, who point to such areas as examples of a broader cultural movement.

It is undeniable that, as the children's saying goes, "Birds of a feather flock together." Those who share characteristics are drawn to one another. This is true for most people in most new settings. Anthropologists have long argued that shared worldviews and cultural models provide humans with the "webs of meaning" that make life predictable.[76] Therefore, it is not surprising that newcomers—who have just uprooted from their homeland and are facing the turmoil of resettling in another—gravitate to one another for a variety of reasons. Social science research suggests that immigrants turn to each other for jobs, information about the new culture, and to share news and reminisce about the old country.[77]

Diane Johnson's novel about a young American woman's extended sojourn in Paris captures the essence of this phenomenon:

> It was restful, in a way, to be in a gathering of American women. No matter what one thinks of one's compatriots, there is undeniably a rapport that cannot be explained. When you meet another American you exchange a glance of understanding. Who you are, your basic cultural assumptions, are known . . . You wouldn't necessarily like these other Americans, but even the ones you didn't like, you always like them better in France then you would like them if you were both back in America.[78]

This experience is true of any expatriate group in a variety of settings. Newcomers will often be seen together and will interact in their more comfortable common language. They speak their language of origin to communicate effectively, not to be rude or to "ir-ritate" others—as one mainstream American informant recently told us. Indeed it would be a rare set of Americans who would speak anything other than English when among themselves in a public set-ting in France, Thailand, or Mexico simply because they were con-cerned about being rude. Much would be lost in the way of sponta-neity and comfort should such a concession to the host society be made.

This is not to say that immigrants do not need to learn to speak the language of the host society. Clearly their very well-being is at stake. Though new immigrants are often accused of not wanting to learn English, in fact enrollments in adult English as a Second Language (ESL) courses are increasing rapidly. Nearly half of the students who participate in adult education classes at the federal, state, and local levels (approximately 1.8 million adults) are enrolled in ESL courses. The demand far exceeds the supply, which results in long waiting lists for hopeful students.[79] As noted Harvard devel-opmental psycholinguist Catherine Snow has found, "Immigrants want to learn English, seek out opportunities to do so, and promote the acquisition of English by their children . . . [English's] status is not endangered by the tiny minority of (mostly elderly) immigrants in the United States who fail to learn it."[80]

Others have charged that the new immigrants are failing to make the symbolically important act of acquiring U.S. citizenship. There was concern that among Mexican-origin immigrants, for example, the rate of application for naturalization (that is, for becoming a cit-izen) was among the lowest of all immigrant groups. The fact that in the late 1990s the INS had received a record number of applica-tions for citizenship from all immigrant groups, including Mexicans, should put this concern to rest. Nearly two million applications for citizenship were submitted in fiscal year 1997—compare that to the 250,000 citizens naturalized in 1993.[81] This phenomenon has had its cynical interpreters who have argued that this wave of new citizens is simply eager to secure publicly funded services that are no longer available to immigrants. For some anti-immigration observers, im-migrants are damned if they do and damned if they don't.

At the very core of the recurring concern that immigrants will not assimilate is the fear that, in the face of the new immigrants' cultural, racial, and linguistic diversity, the mainstream cultural ethos will be impossible to maintain. Some critics argue that while one hundred years ago it was difficult enough to incorporate immigrants from a dozen or so European countries, it is simply impossible to "melt down" the immensely more diverse immigrant population arriving in the United States today. Lost in such pessimistic forecasts is the fact that the values most immigrants carry with them are reminiscent of what used to be described as mainstream American cultural values. Immigrants are first and foremost motivated by economic opportunity, a faith and optimism in a better tomorrow, and strong family ties.

Some new immigrants do maintain some of their more exotic cultural practices, but this has always been true. Earlier waves of immigrants transformed American culture by upgrading our culinary tastes, linguistic practices, and social styles. So today, we have sushi for lunch, talk about the chutzpah of our colleagues, and dance salsa on Saturday night. Plus ça change, plus c'est la même chose!

Perhaps the most important question facing both scholars of immigration and concerned citizens is: Just how is the current wave of immigration both like and unlike the large-scale immigration of a century ago? Are today's Mexicans, Koreans, and Haitians replicating the paths of the Irish, Italian, and Polish immigrants of last century?

The "New" Immigration

What is "new" about the new immigration? The large wave of immigration that began in the 1960s and intensified in the 1990s is referred to by scholars of the discipline as the "new immigration," and its start is often defined by the Hart-Cellar Act of 1965. Since then, well over 20 million immigrants have legally entered the United States. The rate of immigration increased in the 1990s to nearly a million new immigrants per year.

The total number of new immigrants is indeed an impressive (and to some, disconcerting) figure. On the other hand, the proportion of immigrants in the population is approximately 10 percent, well below what it was in the previous historic peak of immigration—the decade between 1900 and 1910—when it approached 15 percent.

The Hart-Cellar Act made family reunification a priority for gaining entry into the United States. American citizens and permanent residents were thus allowed to have their overseas relatives—spouses, children, siblings and others—join them. The other priority of the 1965 act was to recruit immigrants with needed skills and resources. As a result, foreign-born engineers, computer scientists, and investors were welcomed into the United States.

Family reunification and the recruitment of those with skills and resources caused a wave of immigration that has been unprecedented in size and diversity. Today's immigrants are a much more diverse group than ever before in terms of educational background and skills. They are at once among the best-educated and skilled and the least educated and skilled people in the United States. Roughly one-third of all Nobel Prize winners in the United States are immigrants. Fully half of all entering physics graduate students in 1998 were foreign-born.[82] Of all scientists and engineers working in California's famed Silicon Valley, 32 percent are immigrants.[83] Immigrants tend to be overrepresented in the category of people with doctorates just as they are overrepresented among people without high school diplomas. Contrary to popular belief, immigrants today are more educated than in previous eras. Perhaps with the exception of the highly educated immigrants and refugees escaping Nazi Europe, immigrants in the past tended to be more uniformly poorly educated and relatively unskilled than they are today.[84]

Since the Hart-Cellar Act, there has also been a remarkable shift in the countries from which immigrants originate. Prior to 1965, the vast majority of immigrants to the United States had been of European or Canadian origin. Today, the majority emigrate from Latin America, the Caribbean, and Asia (Table 2.1).[85] Hence, they tend to be much more ethnically, socioculturally, and linguistically diverse than before. In recent years, public schools in the two largest U.S. cities (New York and Los Angeles) have enrolled children who speak

Table 2.1   Percentage of foreign-born population by region of origin

Region of origin	1880	1900	1950	1980	1990
Europe	97.0%	93.6%	89.3%	49.6%	25%
Asia	1.6%	1.7%	2.6%	18.0%	25%
Latin America	1.3%	4.2%	6.3%	31.0%	43%
Africa	0.2%	0.4%	1.8%	1.4%	7%

Source: Xue Lan Rong and Judith Preissle, *Educating Immigrant Students* (Thousand Oaks, Calif.: Corwin Press, 1998). Data are from U.S. Census Bureau.

over a hundred different languages. Just thirty years ago, only a dozen or so largely European languages were heard in schoolyards.

Transnational Impulses in the Global Era

Each wave of immigration is part of a larger historic, social, and economic ethos. Each also crystallizes around a dominant theme that comes to capture scholarly attention and the public imagination. The great transatlantic migration has been characterized as a sharp and enduring break with the old country. The young republic, then on the eve of the great industrial expansion, needed large numbers of new workers and consumers. Europeans—especially those imagining expanded opportunities, or facing ethnic and religious persecution—heeded the call and embarked on the journey West, never to look back again.[86]

Some scholars have claimed that this clean break with the old country led to a pattern of steady, progressive assimilation into American society.[87] Countless novels, films, plays, as well as cherished family stories, narrate how poor, illiterate, and often persecuted Italian, Russian, and Irish immigrants "made good" in America. Mario Puzo's book *The Godfather* captured with immense success a somewhat idiosyncratic version of this powerful cultural narrative. In this type of immigration, the second and third generations "assimilate" fully into America and are generously rewarded with wealth and status. In the book, Don Corleone's youngest son becomes a Dartmouth man who, after taking over the "family business," moves to Las Vegas where he attempts to turn his father's criminal mafiosi enterprise into a mainstream business.

This familiar narrative does not seem to fully resonate with today's immigrant stories. Indeed, immigration is now viewed by many in the context of little understood global forces and transnational circuits.[88] Immigrants and their children are now routinely portrayed as actors in an increasingly transnational stage. In the story of the new immigrants, it is said that they not only avoid a sharp break with the country of origin but indeed cultivate transnational ties back home.

The presence of new communication and information technologies as well as the ease of transportation fuels this suspicion that immigrants are not fully incorporating themselves into their new societies. Many immigrants today are said to be at once "here" and "there"—bridging increasingly unbounded national spaces.[89]

According to this view, there is now much more back-and-forth movement than before—not only of people but also of goods, information, and symbols. Irish immigrants of the last century, for example, simply could not have maintained the level and intensity of contact with the old country that is now possible. Immigrants not only reshape the ethos of their new communities, but are also responsible for significant social transformations "back home." Sociologist Peggy Levitt has elegantly documented how among Dominican immigrants in the Northeast "social remittances"—the ideas, values, and interpersonal practices that immigrants acquire in their new homeland—generate important transformations in the lives of those left behind.[90]

According to some portraits, the new immigrants seem to be in perpetual motion, continually shuttling back and forth between the new and the old as if unable to let go of what is good about both countries. Immigrants today are portrayed as relevant actors influencing political processes in both their "new" and "old" lands. Some scholars have noted that the outcome of the most recent Dominican presidential election was largely determined in New York City—where Dominicans are the largest group of new immigrants. Likewise, after years of neglect, Mexican politicians have "discovered" the political value of the seven million Mexican immigrants living in the United States. The new Mexican dual-nationality initiative is also a byproduct of this discovery.

For the children of immigrants, dual nationality can mean shuttling between schools or spending whole summers in the country of origin. While some scholars argue that this transnational strategy is developed in order to maximize opportunities in a global economy, concerned citizens view it as diluting the newcomer's loyalties to their new country.[91] This fear contributes to the anxiety about new immigrants' long-term effect on the cultural fabric of the society.

In general, current characterizations of both the "old" and "new" immigration tend to oversimplify and caricature complex social phenomena. In fact, many European immigrants were quite ambivalent about their place in the new country. A central feature of the great transatlantic immigration from Europe to the Americas from the 1890s until the 1910s was the high proportion of people who returned to Europe. By some accounts, well over one-third of all Europeans who came to the Americas went back "home."[92] Among those who stayed, too, cultural sensibilities were never fully buried in the new land. Eugene O'Neill's acclaimed play of a dysfunctional Irish American family makes the point theatrically: whenever Tyrone's sons speak poorly of his Old World ways, he demands that they leave his beloved Ireland out of their "dirty tongues."[93]

Likewise, the story about how transnationalism is shaping the new immigration is surely more complex than current assumptions and opinions suggest. A general problem in the field is the lack of good data to examine how transnationalism is affecting the everyday lives of immigrant children and families.[94]

Data we have collected for the Longitudinal Immigrant Student Adaptation study suggest that among the new immigrants—and especially among the vast majority of their children—transnationalized contacts with the old country are less intense than many would have predicted. Indeed, our data indicate that there are powerful limitations to the transnationalized contacts that immigrant children can engage in. The distance between countries sharply curtails transnational contacts: travel costs for large families, for example, can be prohibitive. In our sample, only a minority of recent immigrant children had visited their country of origin since they had immigrated.

Legal status is another critical factor affecting whether a child can visit her birthplace. Among children of undocumented status, back and forth visits are infrequent and indeed, practically impossible. Crossing the border illegally is an expensive, dangerous, and stressful experience that few parents want their children to undergo more frequently than is absolutely necessary.

Most of the children in our sample maintain contact with relatives and friends back home.[95] A majority of them rely on telephone calls or letters (though only 7 percent rely solely on letters). Most of the children in our study do not use new information technologies such as the internet and email to keep in touch.[96] Indeed we were surprised that only one child in our study reported using the internet as a way to maintain contact with relatives and friends back home. Ethnicity and parental socioeconomic status are predictably two important factors in who has access to these new communication technologies.[97] So is the issue of the availability of computers with the right programs at the other end of the line—in the country of origin.

While many upper-class professional immigrants of legal status may indeed lead increasingly transnational lives, among children and certainly among immigrants of more limited means, transnationalism seems to be an infrequent rather than overwhelming phenomenon.

Because transnationalism seems to have somewhat less of an influence on the lives of new immigrant children than many have anticipated, it is wise to keep our gaze on the social, economic, and cultural forces that the children are likely to encounter in their new country. In the long term, these factors—more than transnationalism—are likely to shape their life experiences, opportunities, and outcomes.

Most immigrant children, our data suggest, envision themselves settling permanently in the United States. More than half of our participants, adults and children, hoped to live permanently in the

United States, and only 8 percent expressed a preference for going back and forth between the United States and their country of birth.

Joining Postindustrial, Postmodern America

An important aspect of the new immigration is that immigrants and their children are entering a country that is economically, socially, and culturally unlike the country that absorbed—however ambivalently—previous waves of immigrants. Economically, the previous wave to the United States took place on the eve of the great industrial revolution in which, as noted earlier, immigrant workers and consumers played an important role.[98]

Immigrants today are part of a thoroughly globalized, postindustrial economy. An emerging feature of the new economic landscape—the increasing "hourglass" shape of the opportunity structure—is of central relevance to the lives and future of immigrants and their children. On one end of the hourglass, high-skilled immigrants are moving into well-remunerated knowledge-intensive industries at an unprecedented rate.[99] As we noted, fully 32 percent of all information-technology professionals in California's Silicon Valley are immigrants. Never before in the history of U.S. immigration have so many immigrants made the upwardly mobile journey at such a rapid pace.

On the other end of the hourglass economy, large numbers of low-skilled immigrants are entering poorly paid and uninsured service-sector jobs. Unlike the low-skilled factory jobs of yesterday, the kinds of jobs typically available to low-skilled immigrants today do not hold much promise for upward mobility.[100] At the turn of the century, low-skilled immigrant workers with very little formal schooling could, through floor-shop mobility, attain living wages and a comfortable lifestyle. Today's global economy is unforgiving of those without skills and credentials.

Furthermore, low-skill service jobs also fail to provide for the basic needs of a family. Indeed, new research suggests that among new immigrants, a general pattern of declining returns to education means that with more schooling they will be getting fewer rewards in the posteducational opportunity structure than ever before in the history of U.S. immigration.[101] The high school graduate who by-passes college and enters the workforce with no special skills has to-day only a limited advantage over the high school dropout.[102]

The divergence between "low skill" and "high skill" economic spheres is part of a larger pattern of fragmentation characteristic of postindustrial postmodern societies. Indeed, several social theorists have argued that because of an increasing segmentation of the econ-omy and society, large numbers of low-skilled new immigrants are living and working in "environments that have grown increasingly segregated from Whites."[103] As a result, immigrant children are now more likely to attend schools that are more hypersegregated (by both poverty *and* race) than ever before.[104] These tend to be schools that are overcrowded, understaffed, and have outdated curricula.

Distinguished sociologist Alejandro Portes has argued that we can no longer assume that new immigrants will assimilate into a co-herent mainstream. He articulates a critical question that is now in the minds of many observers of immigration:

> The question today is to what sector of American society will a par-ticular immigrant group assimilate? Instead of a relatively uniform "mainstream" whose mores and prejudices dictate a common path of integration, we observe today several distinct forms of adaptation. One of them replicates the time-honored portrayal of growing accul-turation and parallel integration into the white middle class. A sec-ond leads straight in the opposite direction to permanent poverty and assimilation to the underclass. Still a third associates rapid eco-nomic advancement with deliberate preservation of the immigrant community's values and tight solidarity.[105]

The Culture of Multiculturalism

Rather than face a "relatively uniform 'mainstream'" culture, immi-grants today must navigate the complex currents of what we call a "culture of multiculturalism." The cultural models and social prac-tices that we have come to call multiculturalism shape the experi-ences, perceptions, and behavioral repertoires of immigrants in ways not seen in previous eras of large-scale immigration. A hundred years ago there certainly was no culture of multiculturalism that celebrated—however superficially and ambivalently—ethnicity and communities of origin. Indeed, the defining ritual at Ellis Island was the renaming ceremony, when immigration officers—sometimes carelessly and sometimes purposefully—gave new arrivals more Anglicized names in a sort of cultural baptism. Others chose to change their names because of racism, anti-Semitism, or simply to blend in. Hence, Israel Ehrenberg was reborn as Ashley Montague, Meyer Schkolnick became Robert Merton, and Issur Danielovitch Demsky had a new start as Kurt Douglas.[106]

Immigrants today enter social spaces where racial and ethnic categories are important gravitational fields often charged with important political and economic implications. The largest wave of immigration into the United States took place largely after the great struggles of the Civil Rights movement. In that ethos, racial and ethnic categories became powerful shapers of expressive and instrumental ethnicity. By "expressive ethnicity" we mean the feeling of a common origin and a shared destiny with others.[107] These feelings are typically constructed around such phenomena as historic struggles (as in the case of the Serbian sense of peoplehood emerging from their defeat five centuries ago by the Ottomans in the Battle of Kosovo), a common ancestral language (as in the case of the Basques), or religion (as in the case of the Jews in the Diaspora).

By "instrumental ethnicity," we mean the tactical use of ethnicity. In recent years, "identity politics" has become a mode of both expressive self-affirmation and strategic politics. This is in part because ethnic categories have become a critical tool in the workings of the state apparatus. Nation-states create categories for various reasons, such as to count people for census and taxation, or to apportion political representation. Ethnic categories generated by the state are relevant to a variety of civic and political matters; furthermore, they are appropriated and used by various groups for their own strategic needs.

Pan-ethnic categories such as Asian American and Latino have several important features that are relevant for understanding the experiences of immigrants. First, they are largely arbitrary constructions created by demographers and social scientists for data development and analysis. The term "Hispanic," for example, was created by demographers working for the U.S. Bureau of the Census in the 1980s as a way to categorize people who are either historically or culturally connected to the Spanish language. Note that "Hispanic," the precursor to the more au courant term Latino, is a category that has no precise meaning racially or in terms of national origin. Indeed, Latinos are white, black, indigenous and every possible combination of these. They also originate in over twenty countries as varied as Mexico, Argentina, and the Dominican Republic.

Nor do these categories address the sensibilities rooted in these peoples' history and generation in the United States. A Latina, for example, can be a descendant of the original settlers in what is today New Mexico. Although her ancestors spoke Spanish well before English was ever heard on this continent, her family may have resided in this land since before the United States appropriated the Southwest territories. She is considered a Latina just as is a Mayan-speaking arrival from Guatemala who crossed the border last week.

Likewise the term Asian brings together people of highly diverse cultural, linguistic, and religious backgrounds. A Chinese Buddhist and a Filipino Catholic are both considered Asian-American though they may have very little in common in terms of language, cultural identity, and sense of self.

An outcome of our culture of multiculturalism is that new immigrants are pushed to be socialized into becoming "Latino" or "Asian." Although these categories seem to have little resonance with new immigrants as they enter the country, over time they become increasingly relevant, particularly for young adolescents as they begin to struggle developmentally with identity formation. Over the course of our research, we have witnessed the disorientation that immigrant children feel when they discover that their regional, or indeed, national identities have little relevance in the United States. A Taishanese-speaking girl must renegotiate her identity to accommodate the fact that "Asian American" will be her new point of reference. Likewise, a boy from El Salvador will, depending on where he settles, soon discover that what matters now is that he is a Latino and not a Central American or Salvadoran.

In the culture of multiculturalism, identities are created by the person as well as by those around him. Identities are both self-crafted and imposed. Immigrants must come to terms with those impositions. They may include cultural notions of who is a "real American," who is a "successful student," and how one's "color and race" fit into existing ethnic categories. Based on shared cultural stereotypes, a person is told both what she "must be" and what she "cannot be." Thus, a fourth-generation Japanese American who proudly serves in the U.S. military is outraged when asked by people in the street—while in uniform—whether he is in the "Chinese Army." The message he hears is that he "can't be a real American." The Latina student in the advanced placement calculus class is routinely told by her classmates that she "must be" Asian—the stereotype of the successful minority student. The dark-skinned Dominican is told that he cannot be Latino—he "must be" black.

The question those interested in the new immigration must ask is whether in the long term the anxieties and stereotypes about today's new immigrants will dissipate over time as they did for past European immigrants. The children of immigrants of European origin could "disappear" into the mainstream by changing their names and losing their accents. Will this option be available to the children of today's immigrants of color? Will people who visibly look, talk, dress, and move differently be allowed to truly become members of their new societies? Will what it means to be an American be transformed into a more elastic and inclusive notion than it seems to be in its current form? The verdict is still out, but undoubtedly it is a challenge that as a society we must embrace.

3

THE PSYCHOSOCIAL
EXPERIENCE OF IMMIGRATION

Families migrate to improve their lives. For many, immigration results in opportunity, and personal growth. But there are costs involved in all immigrant journeys. Immigration is a transformative process with profound implications for the family. Immigrant children experience a particular constellation of changes that have lasting effects upon their development. And yet surprisingly little systematic research has focused on the psychological experiences of immigrant children.[1] Much of the work to date has either emphasized the adult immigrant experience or has examined the physical rather than psychological health of children. What do we really know about what it is like to be a child in a new country?

Separations and Reunification

Many new immigrants migrate primarily to be reunited with family members who emigrated earlier. Family networks generate—and sustain—substantial migratory flows. Indeed, transnational family reunification continues to be a critical factor in immigration today.[2] While a number of studies have examined how transnational family chains generate a powerful momentum of their own, we know little about how children manage the complex social and psychological experiences that come under the rubric of "family reunification."

For many immigrant children today, family reunification is a long, painful, and disorienting ordeal. Only 20 percent of the children in our sample came to the United States as a family unit. Most of the children were separated from one or both parents for a few

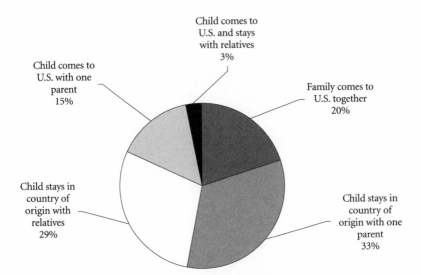

Figure 3.1 Immigration and separation from parents. Such separations may not be harmful if they are considered normal in the child's native culture and if the child has healthy relationships with the parents and family members providing care.

months to a few years. Figure 3.1 includes the various ways that immigrant children are separated from their parents during the family's migration.

Immigrant children respond in a variety of ways to their separations from loved family members. For some, not surprisingly, it is a traumatic process. Others find it stressful but not traumatic. How the children experience the separation, their social conditions back home, and their perceptions of what is going on plays a critical role in their subsequent adaptations in the new land.

The cultural frame for the separation will influence how the child internalizes and responds to the experience. For example, in Caribbean countries there is a long-standing cultural practice of "child fostering." Children are sent to live with relatives either purposefully (as in when a mother has a live-in work position or when educational opportunities are better near a relative) as well as in response to a family crisis. In that social context, the separation is often *not* experienced as abandonment. When international separations occur, however, expectations in the host culture are likely to have important repercussions—especially when children enter a new social context where such separations are viewed as a symptom of a pathological family situation.[3] Teachers, administrators, physicians, and other professionals often misinterpret the social meanings of these separations and are quick to label absent parents as not caring about or being properly attached to their children. Receiving such social signals may complicate the child's interpretations and psychological responses to the separation. The child may begin to doubt that her parents had her best interests in mind.

When the separation is not protracted, is carefully planned, and when the child has a clear understanding of what will happen next, the process may be not harmful to the child. This certainly is true if the child is well cared for by loving relatives during the separation. It is also important that the parents maintain regular communication and give frequent updates about the anticipated reunification. Communication can take the form of phone calls, letters and postcards, audio or videotapes, photographs, and gifts. Children reported feeling touched and "special" when they received precious gifts from their parents prior to joining them. Haitian novelist Edwidge Danticat reveals how the packages sent to children carry emotions as well as gifts: "Around us were dozens of other people trying to squeeze all their love into small packets to send back home."[4]

Even under the best of conditions, however, there will be losses and ambivalence. If the child was left with a loving caretaker for an extended period of time, she will become attached to that caretaker. The beloved aunt or grandmother may assume the role of symbolic mother. Danticat, who was left behind by her mother with her loving aunt in Haiti, recalls how she felt that she was "my mother's daughter and Tante Atie's child."[5] When a child leaves to join the parents, she will probably feel both happy about the prospect of "regaining" them and disappointed about losing close contact with her beloved caretakers.

For children who are left for long periods with more ambivalent relatives who are neglectful or even abusive, there are more serious problems. This situation is exacerbated if the child has no clear timetable or sense of what will happen next, and little or no communication with parents.

Once the child does migrate to reunite with her family, all kinds of delicate psychological adjustments will be required. If the separation was long, the reunited family must first get reacquainted. And when the reunification involves children who were left behind when very young, the child will in essence be "meeting" her parents.

If new younger siblings are born during the separation, the older child who was "left behind" will almost inevitably have to contend with feelings of jealousy and disconnection with the family unit. In many cases, too, parental authority needs to be renegotiated—before, grandma and grandpa were the disciplinarians, and now the child may have to deal with a new set of rules. Indeed, many immigrant children reported to us that with the move they experienced a significant loss of freedom because immigrant parents are often very concerned about crime in their new neighborhoods.

Much will depend on whether the child left behind felt neglected and abandoned or, conversely, viewed the separation as necessary to the future well-being of the family. If a child felt neglected, "acting out" upon reunification may be a way to "punish" parents for leaving him behind. While most children are happy to be reunited with their families, they are also likely to feel disoriented and even depressed while they mourn their lost attachments: their best friends, beloved grandparents, or a favorite aunt left behind. For these children, the gains of immigration are tainted by loss.

The Stresses of Immigration

Transitions are always stressful. Social scientists and mental health professionals have long regarded events like moves, job changes, and ruptures in social relations as highly disruptive.[6] Transitions can trigger a variety of reactions, including excitement, anticipation, and hope as well as anxiety, anger, depression, somatic complaints, and illness.[7]

Transitions become particularly stressful when people are both unable to draw on their usual resources and coping strategies and are conscious of just how much is at stake.[8] Immigration often captures both of these elements. It is a major life transition where the stakes are high. Because families consciously choose to invest precious resources in the move, failure to adapt in the new setting can lead to serious consequences.

Indeed, by any measure, immigration is one of the most stressful events a family can undergo.[9] It removes family members from many of their relationships and a predictable context: community ties, jobs, customs, and (often) language. Immigrants are stripped of many of their significant relationships—extended family members, best friends, and neighbors. They also lose the social roles that provide them with culturally scripted notions of how they fit into the world. Initially, without a sense of competence, control, and belonging, many immigrants will feel marginalized. These changes in relationships, contexts, and roles are highly disorienting and nearly inevitably lead to a keen sense of loss.[10]

At the most dramatic end of the stress spectrum are the events that result in post-traumatic stress disorder (PTSD). Experiencing or witnessing killing, rape, or torture often leads to transient as well as long-term symptoms.[11] Asylum seekers from Kosovo, Bosnia, Somalia, Central America, Vietnam, and Haiti have often escaped from highly traumatic situations. PTSD symptoms include recurrent traumatic memories, a general numbing of responses, as well as a persistent sense of increased arousal leading to intense anxiety, irritability, outbursts of anger, difficulty concentrating, and insomnia.[12] New arrivals who have experienced trauma will often suffer recurring waves of symptoms and remain preoccupied with the violence they left behind. In addition to recurring thoughts, images, and nightmares of painful past events, they may feel guilty about having escaped when loved ones remain behind.[13]

These symptoms add significantly to the stresses of immigration. To complicate matters, traumatized new arrivals in need of counseling can seldom communicate with ease in the new language. They must face a whole array of challenges in the new setting often without cultural competence or the necessary social supports. The severity of the symptoms will in many ways depend on the extent of the trauma as well as the psychological, social, and material resources available to the victims in the new setting.

Other immigrants face a different form of violence as they cross the border. The actual border crossing is often extremely frightening and upsetting for adults and children alike. Undocumented crossers at the U.S.-Mexican border are subject to a variety of dangers including exposure to heat exhaustion as well as violence at the hands of border agents, "coyotes" (paid crossing guides), and others. Girls and women face additional risks. According to a recent disturbing Amnesty International report, "women are at particular risk of being physically abused, raped, robbed, or murdered on their journey."[14]

Our own interviews with immigrant children reveal that many of them experience the crossing of the border as highly traumatic. Some were detained, deported, beaten, or humiliated. Others sensed potential danger. A nine-year-old Mexican boy with fear in his voice told us of his crossing: "I had to be careful of where I put my feet. My parents told me that the *migra* [slang term for the INS] had put piranhas in the river to keep us away."[15]

Immigrant families who survive the violence of their countries and the crossing ironically often find a new form of violence as they settle in their American neighborhoods. New arrivals today, especially those from Latin America and the Caribbean, tend to settle in highly segregated neighborhoods where violence is an everyday occurrence.[16] All too many immigrant children experience disconcertingly high levels of violence in their new neighborhood and school settings. Of our informants, 36 percent indicated that violence was the thing they liked least about living in the United States. An eleven-year-old Mexican girl told us: "There is a lot of violence here in the United States. They kill people in the streets." A thirteen-year-old Mexican girl said: "There I was freer. Here there are bad people who hurt children." A twelve-year-old Haitian girl recounted: "I don't like the neighborhood where I live. There is a lot of crime in the neighborhood. One day, we were sleeping and the police came and opened the door. There was a man in the apartment above us who had killed his wife . . . I was scared because he could have come and killed us too." A ten-year-old Mexican boy reported a frightening incident: "I saw a man lying out in front of my house with blood on his legs and stomach. I think someone shot him." Another child, a thirteen-year-old Chinese girl, told us: "I have seen gang activities near my house . . . I am afraid to go out—I don't feel safe."

Surely not all immigrants experience violence or trauma either in their homeland or in their new land. Many fly in comfortable airplanes, are politely received by INS officers, and move into safe middle-class neighborhoods. Nonetheless, it is important to bear in mind that for a significant number of immigrant children, violence has been and continues to be a part of their lives.

Even when violence is not a defining feature of the immigrant experience, immigrant families endure other forms of stress. While anticipating the migration and during the first weeks in the new country, many experience a sense of euphoria.[17] Expectations are often high; for many the anticipated possibilities seem boundless. Upon arrival, immigrants focus their energies on attending to the immediate needs of settling into the new environment. The priorities include finding a place to live, securing employment, and enrolling the children in schools. There is little time for the family to process psychologically many aspects of their new experiences.

After taking care of the essential needs, immigrants will begin to confront some unanticipated realities. Many will experience a variety of psychological problems.[18] Most frequently, the cumulative losses of loved ones and familiar contexts will lead to a range of feelings, from mild sadness to depression to "perpetual mourning."[19] For others, the general dissonance in cultural expectations and the loss of predictable context will be experienced as anxiety and an acute disorientation.[20] Many immigrants who arrive with exaggerated expectations of opportunity and wealth must come to terms with a starker reality. Disappointed aspirations, when coupled with a hostile reception in the new environment, may lead some to feelings of distrust, suspicion, anger, and even paranoia.[21] While some immigrants will display acute symptoms that should be treated, others—

perhaps most—feel only transient discomfort and adapt to their circumstances with relative ease.

Learning the New Rules

A form of stress specific to immigration is referred to as "acculturation stress."[22] Acculturation is the process of learning new cultural rules and interpersonal expectations. Language is not the only form of communication that immigrants must learn. Social interactions are culturally structured. A Middle Eastern immigrant will need to learn that in the United States, most people stand farther apart when speaking than in her native country. Argentines will need to learn that Americans will interpret their normal volume in discussion as near shouting. A Haitian child will sooner or later find out that politely averting her eyes while her teacher is scolding her (as her parents taught her) will only anger her American teacher more. A Brazilian immigrant will need to learn the culture of "appointments"— in her new country, a nine o'clock appointment does not mean arriving anytime between nine and eleven. All immigrants must learn the new rules of engagement.

Such cultural practices are first learned in childhood as part of socially shared repertoires that make the flow of life predictable. The social flow changes in dramatic ways following immigration. As Polish immigrant Eva Hoffmann describes in her exquisitely written memoirs, immigration causes people to fall "out of the net of meaning into the weightlessness of chaos."[23] Without a sense of cultural competence, control, and belonging, immigrants are often left with a keen sense of loss and disorientation. A twenty-three-year-old Mexican informant summed up the experience: "I became an infant again. I had to learn all over again to eat, to speak, to dress, and what was expected of me."

Immigrant children typically come into contact with American culture sooner and, indeed more intensely, than their parents do. Schools are an important site of cultural contact for immigrant children. It is where they meet teachers (who are often members of the dominant culture) as well as children from other backgrounds. For many immigrant children today, peers will be members of other ethnic and racial minorities.[24] In schools they must contend quickly and intensively with the new culture. Their parents, however, may be more removed from mainstream American culture, particularly if they work, as many do, in jobs with other immigrants and those of the same ethnic background.[25] The child's fast absorption into the new culture will create particular conflicts and tensions.[26] Children may have feelings ranging from vague to intense embarrassment in regard to aspects of their parents' "old country" and "old-fashioned" ways. Parents may try to slow down the process by warning children not to act like other children in the new setting.

As a result of their greater exposure to the new culture, children often learn the new language more quickly than do their parents. Though the child may continue to speak the home language, the level of fluency is likely to atrophy over time. Without a concerted effort by both parents and children, the vocabulary and literacy level of the language of origin usually lags far behind that of the new language. While the child may easily communicate about basic needs in her language of origin ("What is for dinner?"), she is likely to have more difficulty communicating subtleties of thought and emotion in that language.[27] Parents, however, often continue to communicate more effectively in the language of origin. Hence in complex discussions between parents and children, subtleties of meanings are likely to be missed and miscommunication may result. It is not uncommon to overhear discussions in which parents and children switch back and forth between languages and completely miss one another's intent. Esmeralda Santiago recalls the special linguistic bond she developed with her siblings—and how her mother and grandmother were excluded: "Slowly, as our vocabularies grew, it became a bond between us, one that separated us from Tata and from Mami, who watched us perplexed, [their] expression changing from pride, to envy to worry."[28] The worry may not be misplaced. Children are not above deliberately using their linguistic edge to mislead their parents. A thirteen-year-old Mexican boy admitted to us that he had told his parents that the *F* on his report card stood for "fabulous."

Family Roles

Migration tends to have a destabilizing effect on the family.[29] It creates particular stresses on the family system that may translate into conflict between family members, particularly if there were tensions prior to migration. For example, migration often reduces the amount of time that parents and children spend together. Many immigrant parents (particularly those coming from poorer backgrounds) work several jobs. These and other obligations make them less available. Immigrant parents often tell us that working hard is the best way they can help their children, yet these long work hours leave many children unattended. This physical absence compounds the psychological unavailability that often accompanies parental anxiety and depression.[30] These two forms of absence all too frequently leave immigrant children to their own devices long before they are develpmentally ready. While in some cases this leads to hyper-responsible children, in other cases it leads to depressed kids who are drawn to the lure of alternative family structures such as gangs.[31]

Migration creates other changes within the structure of the family. Children who learn English more quickly than their parents are placed in situations where they must advocate for them. They may become privy to "family secrets" in their new roles as translators in medical, legal, and other social settings. Roles are often reversed, turning culturally scripted dynamics of parental authority upside down. Lan Cao, a Vietnamese refugee who arrived as a child, captures these dynamics poignantly:

> The dreadful truth was simply this: we were going through life in reverse, and I was the one who would help my mother through the hard scrutiny of ordinary suburban life. I would have to forgo the luxury of adolescent experiments and temper tantrums, so that I could scoop my mother out of harm's way and give her sanctuary. Now, when we stepped into the exterior world, I was the one who told my mother what was acceptable and unacceptable behavior . . . And even though I hesitated to take on the responsibility, I had no choice.

It was not a simple process, the manner in which my mother relinquished motherhood. The shift in status occurred not just in the world but in the safety of our home as well, and it became most obvious when we entered the realm of language.[32]

More than simple issues of relative linguistic competence are at work in the complex mutual familial calibrations that immigration requires. Former family leaders may be "demoted."[33] A wise grandfather who in Hong Kong is the source of guidance may now be unable to give meaningful practical advice to his granddaughter. Because immigrant parents "have no map of experience" before them, their self-assurance and authority can be undermined both in the outside world as well as in the more intimate world of the family.[34]

Parental loss of status in the new society has profound effects on the morale of the parent and hence the child. Luis Alberto Urrea describes the collapsing status his father experienced as he moved from the upper echelons of Mexican politics and power to the demeaning role of "greaser" in San Diego, California: "Nothing broke my father. Except for the U.S. He couldn't find his footing here. He couldn't rise again, and he knew it. He tried many jobs—busboy, cannery worker, bakery truck driver. I often think that he settled on bowling alleys because he was the most erudite man there, even if he was a greaser."[35]

Within the intimacy of the family, "the worm of self-doubt that undermines basic certitude" likewise subverts parental authority.[36] Eva Hoffman recalled about her parents following the family's migration from Poland: "They don't try to exercise much influence over me. 'In Poland, I would have known how to bring you up, I would have known what to do,' my mother says wistfully, but here she has lost her sureness, her authority."[37]

While some parents may quietly relinquish their authority, others resist doing so and may become severe disciplinarians. But the ways that immigrant parents discipline their children also may have to do with child-rearing practices in their country of origin. Withholding a meal, spanking a child, or pulling a child's ear are not uncommon techniques found in many countries, but they are dissonant with

mainstream American ideals of the proper disciplining
parents discipline their children in ways approved of iⁱ
try of origin, they may come into conflict with U.S. Chⁱ
Services.[38]

In other cases, disciplinary practices seem to be secondary to the
stresses generated by the migration itself. As parents are frustrated
and feel increasingly threatened by the encroachment of new cultural values and behaviors among their children, they often attempt
to "tighten the reins." But the children, wise to the ways of the new
land, may use against their parents the threat of reporting them to
state agencies. This further debilitates parental authority. In the Haitian community, it is said that "the first thing a child learns in the
United States is to dial 911." In another folkloristic story, it was said
that as soon as a Salvadorian father returned to the Central America
for a visit with his family, he spanked his son "for all the times I
could not spank you in the United States." While these stories probably contain only a grain of truth, during the course of our research
many parents indeed reported to us their frustrations and fears of
state encroachment into their basic parental authorities. Many fear
that in the new country, laws and customs will prevent them from
ensuring that their children behave in ways they deem appropriate.

Gender and the New Culture

Immigrant families are often caught in powerful and contradicting
social currents, which result in both radical change and regidificat-
ion. In the realm of gender relations, many of the paradoxes created
by immigration appear with clarity and force. Immigration sets in
motion certain forces that draw women away from the inner world
of the family. Economic necessity dictates that women venture (in
many cases for the first time) into the world of work outside of the
home.[39] By venturing out of the world of the family and into the
world of work and the new culture, immigrant women often adapt
more quickly in subtle ways that have important implications for
family life.

At the same time, a powerful counterforce gives immigrant women the responsibility for maintaining the traditions, values, and

norms of the country of origin. In the upheaval of immigration, women typically emerge as the keepers of culture and family traditions. While some women become the self-appointed guardians of tradition, others may feel that this role is imposed upon them by their husbands and other members of the community.[40] Many immigrant families fear the detrimental affects of "Americanization" should the mother fail to act as cultural guardian. Rumors and other informal and formal social sanctions will be levied against women who fail to control the influences of Americanization on, for example, their sons' or daughters' style of dress, dating, and progress in school.

These pervasive dynamics generate their own opportunities and tensions. In the long term, many women come to experience immigration as liberating. It may result in more equitable gender relations, social freedom, and empowerment. Indeed, researchers have found that immigrant women are more likely than their husbands to feel content with their new situations and are less likely to say that they wish to return to their homeland.[41]

Recently arrived women often work in jobs that place them in intimate and sustained contact with members of the dominant society. They may find employment as child-care workers, in elderly care, and as housekeepers. As such, many enter the homes of members of the dominant society and become privy to different gender relations, child-rearing techniques, and expectations about the future. As they observe and evaluate new cultural models and social practices, they may subtly act as catalysts to change within their own families. In the long term, women must strike a balance between promoting certain forms of change they find desirable and guarding against those forms of change they perceive as harmful.

As immigrant women craft new roles and enjoy newfound independence, tensions within the husband-wife relationship may occur. For men, the adjustments can be difficult. Conflicts are most likely to occur when the wife's gains coincide with a social demotion for the husband—for example, when he is unemployed or can only find work beneath his qualifications and skills. As a result, spousal abuse is an issue in some immigrant families.[42]

Immigrant families make a Faustian bargain. While the long-term goal of immigration is greater opportunity for the children, parents often panic when their children begin to show the first signs of Americanization. Many immigrant families encourage their children to pick up certain cultural competencies (such as the English language) while fiercely resisting others. They come to see certain American attitudes and behaviors as a threat to family unity. They often view American popular culture as wanting in such realms as dating, respect of elders, and peer relations. Immigrant parents view with suspicion even such cultural icons as slumber parties; many of our informants reported that their parents would never allow them to sleep over at a friend's house.

Esmeralda Santiago recalls her mother's ambivalence: "The way she pronounced *Americanized,* it sounded like a terrible thing, to be avoided at all costs, another *algo* to be added to the list of 'somethings' outside the door . . . It was good to be healthy, big, and strong like Dick, Jane, and Sally. It was good to learn English and to know how to act among Americans, but it was not good to behave like them."[43]

Nowhere are the anxieties around Americanization more clearly articulated than in parental concerns about their daughters' exposure to the cultural repertoire of the American peer group. In some immigrant communities, becoming "Americanized" is synonymous with becoming sexually promiscuous.[44] Often significant family tensions emerge around the dating of adolescent girls. As a result, the activities of girls outside the home tend to be heavily monitored and controlled. While boys may be encouraged to venture into the new world, girls and young women are more likely to be kept close to the family hearth. Because girls tend to value social and family ties more than their brothers, they may be reluctant to struggle to separate from the family.[45] Adolescent girls often experience the burden of being torn between the pursuit of romantic love and the role of dutiful daughter.[46]

Immigrant girls have far more responsibilities at home than do their brothers.[47] Their roles include translating; advocating in financial, medical, legal transactions; and acting as surrogate parents with younger siblings. Eldest children in particular are expected to assist with such tasks as babysitting, feeding younger siblings, getting siblings ready for school in the morning, and escorting them to school.[48]

As a result of the concerns around dating and the heavy family responsibilities at home, activities of immigrant girls outside the home are heavily restricted. These restrictions are often experienced by adolescent girls as "unfair" and "oppressive" and may be the focus of family conflict. Immigration researcher Rob Smith and his team at Columbia University, however, note that these restrictions seem to protect girls somewhat from violence or gang-related activities. Indeed, several researchers have found that girls are less likely to be involved in gangs, and when they are, their involvement is more symbolic and less intense.[49] Girls who flirt with gang activities are more likely to remain in school and to transition relatively smoothly out of gangs and into the labor market.[50] A major related finding indicates that substance abuse is substantially lower in immigrant girls than boys.[51] Immigrant girls are also less likely than their native-born counterparts to engage in substance abuse and other risky behaviors.[52]

In schools, immigrant girls tend to outperform immigrant boys. Since the beginning of this century, among most ethnic groups, immigrant girls tended to complete more years of school than their male counterparts.[53] An analysis of census data found that Asian American females reach higher levels of educational attainment than males.[54] In a study of Caribbean-origin youth in New York City, the eminent Harvard immigration scholar Mary Waters found that girls are more likely than boys to complete high school.[55]

While immigrant girls tend to outperform their brothers in school, there are some exceptions.[56] Religion and culture have a tremendous influence on the experiences of immigrant girls. Girls of Hindi Indian or Muslim Afghani backgrounds face very different issues than do Catholic Mexican, or Buddhist Chinese, girls. Arranged marriages are the norm in some cultures—for a girl raised in a postindustrial culture steeped in media images of what life should be like in the new society, this practice will cause much more emotional conflict than if she had been raised in her country of origin.[57] Among those immigrant families that discourage their daughters from remaining in school past marriageable age (which may be in their mid-teens), educational pursuits for girls will be cut short.

On aggregate, however, immigrant girls tend to have more successful educational careers than boys do. Why? Several reasons are at work. Because immigrant girls are more restricted by their parents than are boys, "time at school . . . becomes a precious social experience."[58] They tend to view their time in school as a period of relative freedom (in contrast to mainstream American teenagers, who tend to talk about school as a "prison experience.")[59] They may feel more positive about school and therefore may be more seriously engaged in learning.

Girls and boys seem to respond somewhat differently to cultural and racial stereotypes. As eminent anthropologists George De Vos and John Ogbu have noted, academic engagement is compromised for youth coming from stigmatized backgrounds.[60] But boys from these groups have even more problems performing in school than do the girls. This seems to be the case, for example, among Caribbean-origin youth in Britain, Canada, and the United States, among North African males in Belgium, and among Moroccan and Algerian boys in France.[61]

In addition, Harvard psychiatrist Felton Earls has persuasively argued that familial and community control play a significant role in the well-being (including academics) of youth.[62] Furthermore, teachers' expectations for minority boys are quite different than those for girls. Teachers and administrators often perceive adolescent minority and immigrant boys as threatening. Another contribution to the gender gap may be the strong peer pressure for boys to reject school.[63] Behaviors that gain respect with peers often bring boys in conflict with their teachers.

Influences on Successful Long-Term Adaptation

In all social systems, the family is a basic structural unit, the most significant emotional foundation in the lives of individuals. This is especially so for immigrants who may not have other social networks immediately available to them. Understanding family-level factors is indeed critical for evaluating the long-term adaptations of immigrant children. In looking at the role of immigrant families, however, we must be cautious. Immigrant families are structured in a variety of culturally relative ways. In some cases, the nuclear family (father-mother-children) is the ideal type. In other cases, however, matrifocal patterns (where women are at the center of family life) are the norm. In still other immigrant families, extended members such as grandparents, aunts, and uncles are integral to the system. It is therefore always risky to apply mainstream, middle-class standards to immigrant family dynamics.[64]

Family cohesion and the maintenance of a well-functioning system of supervision, authority, and mutuality are perhaps the most powerful factors in shaping the well-being and future outcomes of all children—immigrant and nonimmigrant alike. Because no family is an island, family cohesion and healthy dynamics are enhanced when the family is part of a larger community that displays effective forms of what Felton Earls has termed "community agency."[65]

Patterns of social cohesion and belonging can be assessed by a variety of social indicators. Perhaps the most important of these is: Who is in charge in the life of a child? Are the parents and other responsible adults in control of children's activities, or are the peers most influential? Do the adults know what the children are up to? Does information about potential trouble travel through the community network before it is too late and the police become involved? Do parents know the parents of their children's friends?

Factors relating to parents' socioeconomic and educational background also influence the adaptations of immigrant families: they play a decisive role in determining the kinds of neighborhoods that families settle into, the kinds of schools that children attend, and the ability to maintain contact with loved ones back home by making regular visits.[66] On the whole, upper-middle-class immigrants are able to retain much of their prestige and offer their children better opportunities. Individuals and families of middle- and lower-class backgrounds are likely to face more adverse circumstances, to settle into less desirable neighborhoods, and to enroll their children in schools with fewer resources. They will also have fewer opportunities to visit their country of origin and so may suffer from being cut off from their loved ones.

Middle-class immigrants often experience significant losses in prestige: they frequently find employment in positions far below their training and qualifications because of language difficulties, lack of connections, or lack of certification in certain professions. The high school teacher from Moscow becomes a babysitter; the Indian doctor a preschool teacher; the Haitian lawyer a cab driver. In addition, middle-class immigrants may suffer for the first time the painful experience of prejudice and discrimination in the new country.

The poorest immigrants, who are largely members of the lower classes in their country of origin, often suffer tremendous adversity as a result of immigration. In spite of these difficulties—which may include xenophobia, racism, and fierce competition for the least desirable jobs—they often improve their economic and social circumstances. In addition, while they certainly suffer from discrimination in the new country, social disparagement may not necessarily be a new experience. As members of the lower socioeconomic class, they are likely to have suffered such treatment in their country of origin. They have less to lose and less far to fall. Those with little or no education, however, find themselves at a great disadvantage in guiding their children through the complex educational maze in the new land.

While the family is extremely important to how the child adapts to the new land, a number of other factors significantly shape how children respond to the transitions and stresses of immigration.[67] Some of these factors involve characteristics that immigrant families bring with them, and others involve variables they encounter in the new land.

The circumstances surrounding the migration can play a key role. Was the family pushed or pulled out of the country of origin? If the family was lured out of the homeland by the promise of opportunity and adventure, its members are likely to be more positively disposed to the experience than if they were pushed out by ethnic, religious, or political conflict, chronic hardship, or famine. By the same token, at least initially, the individual initiating the migration is likely to be more enthusiastic about the experience than a reluctant spouse, elderly parent, or child.[68] We have found that children in particular often have only a vague understanding of why the family is migrating. As a result, they may not look forward to the migration and may experience the move as an imposition from which they have little to gain.

Personality and temperamental factors make a great difference too.[69] A healthy response to dramatic change requires the ability to adapt to new circumstances. Individuals who are rigid in their views, or who have a high need for predictability, are likely to suffer.[70] Those who are particularly shy, proud, or sensitive to outside opinions are also at higher risk, as are those who are highly suspicious of the motivations of others. Being able to draw upon a variety of coping strategies is certainly an important asset.[71]

By the same token, psychological and physical health prior to migration will also aid or impede the ease of the response to immigration. Children who are suffering from post-traumatic stress (as discussed earlier) are of course highly at risk. So too, are immigrants who suffer from depressive tendencies as well as any number of other psychiatric disorders. Physical health may also play a role, particularly if an illness or disability interferes with either maintaining gainful employment or with general quality of life.

Speaking the language of the new country clearly is an asset. Religiosity and connection with a church may also play a positive role. On the other hand, moving from a village to a major city (a common pattern for many immigrants) may complicate the transition. Many immigrant children in our study report to us that they find it very difficult to adjust to the *encerramiento* (Spanish for being "shut in"). While they may have had considerable freedom to play and roam their neighborhoods in their place of origin, they often lose such freedoms when moving to an urban environment.

Once in the new setting, the network of social relations is important. Nothing is better for one's mental health than having friends and family. The relative absence of social support has been linked to disease, mortality, slowed recovery, and mental illness. The presence of a healthy social support network has long been regarded as a key mediator of stress.[72]

Interpersonal relationships are important in several ways.[73] Immigrants, disoriented in the new land, rely on friends and relatives to provide them with tangible aid (such as running an errand or making a loan) as well as guidance and advice (including job and housing leads). The companionship of these friends and relatives also helps maintain and enhance self-esteem and provides much needed acceptance and approval. A well-functioning social support network, quite predictably, is closely linked to better adjustment to the new environment. Of course, in part, the availability of an effective social support structure will be influenced by the individual's preexisting social competence. Individuals with highly developed social skills are likely to be better able to establish and draw upon interpersonal relationships.[74]

A number of other factors in the new setting must be considered in understanding the adaptation of the immigrants. Whether or not the immigrant is "documented" or "undocumented" will affect his or her access to opportunities and general quality of life.[75]

For adults the availability of jobs will be key. Here, social networks will be important because employers often rely on migrant networks to provide them with referrals to potential new employees.[76] Features of the job itself—wages, seasonal availability, safety, and pleasantness of the work—will also play a role in the employee's adjustment.

For children, the quality of their schools will ease or complicate the transition. Unfortunately, many immigrant children find themselves in segregated, poor, and conflict-ridden schools.[77] In our sample of schools, several administrators have reported high crime rates. In one of our participating middle schools, a student was raped and murdered; a high school principal told us of approximately thirty murders during the previous year within the immediate neighborhood; and many other school officials and students complained of significant gang activity on school property and in the surrounding neighborhood. A middle school student told us that a security guard, who had supposedly been hired to protect the students, was the main dealer of drugs on campus. During focus groups we conducted with Mexican immigrant students in a San Francisco Bay Area school, students said that only a few days earlier an escaped prisoner had barricaded himself during school hours on the school grounds, leading to an exchange of gunshots between him and the police.[78]

Obviously, neighborhood safety will do much to influence the quality of life for children and adults alike. Many immigrants move to inner-city areas in search of housing that they can afford. Unfortunately, affordable urban housing is often located in areas that are virtual war zones.

Finally, as we discussed in the previous chapter, the way that immigrant children are received plays a critical role in their adaptation. As we outlined, discrimination against many new immigrants is widespread, and social scientists have established that prejudice and exclusion are traumatic.[79] Exclusion can be structural (such as when individuals are kept from jobs or housing) or attitudinal (as when new arrivals are treated with disparagement and public hostility). It impinges upon the daily quality of life of its victims and interferes with their emotional health and social adaptation.[80] In the long term, xenophobia and exclusion can deeply undermine the immigrant child's trust in equal opportunity and hope for the future.

Immigrant families and their children face multiple challenges. While the special problems we have delineated in this chapter are part of their daily lives, most immigrant families cope well with the stresses. For most, the acute phase of distress is limited in severity and short-lived. Over time, as these immigrants become more acclimatized and less disoriented—a task that is easier for those who are able to settle in well-functioning close-knit communities—many will thrive. Most immigrants will find that overall, their gains outweigh their losses.

4

REMAKING IDENTITIES

Especially early on, much of immigration is a process of comparing the "here and now" with the "there and then." Immigrants frequently leave behind a host of difficulties, and although in the new land other challenges are ever present, the old troubles may make the new ones tolerable. This dual frame of reference acts as a perceptual filter by which the newcomers process their new experiences.[1] Everything from their pay, quality of life at work, and the schooling of the children is framed in comparative terms. As we walk through a library in an inner-city urban school, a Salvadoran mother said: "Look at all of these wonderful books! Here you get them for free; there we had to buy our own."

Immigrant parents also typically bring with them a sense of optimism about how their hard work will open new opportunities. Hope is in the heart of every immigrant. Possibilities for the future—especially for their children—appear obvious. At the same time immigrants are preoccupied daily with the mundane tasks required to survive and forge ahead. The immigration process consumes nearly all the psychological and physical energies of immigrant parents.

The objective conditions of many immigrants may be difficult or even intolerable by the standards of native-born Americans. But immigrants' dual frame of reference makes them optimistic about the future. Most come to experience their living and working situation as tolerable and indeed preferable to that which they have left behind. This mindset allows them to resiliently face the challenges of immigration.

What holds true for the parents may not hold true for their children. Those born and raised abroad may share a number of characteristics with their parents—a dual frame of reference, an appreciation for new opportunities, and a general optimism about the future. But the children of immigrants who arrived when they were very young or who were born here will not have the same clear-cut frame of reference against which to measure their current situation. Rather than using their parents' standard, they apply the new society's expectations about lifestyles and quality of living. Although they may not come to experience the standards of the American lifestyle first-hand, store windows, television, movies, and an occasional visit to the home of a more privileged peer may show them what life can be here—and what they are not getting. Many of these children may feel deprived in relation to the more affluent lifestyles of the mainstream culture.

Seductive television and movie images, as well as the habits and ambitions of their native-born peers, provide powerful models of possible lifestyles and the "American Dream." Paradoxically, at this moment in history, when the country is struggling with some anxiety about its ability to culturally withstand the latest wave of new immigrants, American culture itself is arguably at its most powerful and influential moment on the worldwide stage. Through new information technologies, the American ethos dominates youth culture, influencing language, street fashions, and music worldwide. From Paris to Katmandu to La Paz, youth are wearing hip-hop clothing, watching MTV, and standing in lines to see the same movies.

Even before the American dominance of international youth culture, the children of immigrants have always gravitated to characteristics of the new culture. Children quickly acquire new language skills and often become reluctant to speak their original language in public. They desperately want to wear clothes that will let them be "cool" or, at the very least, do not draw attention to themselves as "different." Children of immigrants become acutely aware of nuances of behaviors that although "normal" at home, will set them apart as "strange" and "foreign" in public.

While immigrant parents generally acquire some English skills, it is likely that they "never really catch on to how different the rules are here."[2] Children of immigrants, on the other hand, are likely to learn the rules of the game quickly and easily. These children are drawn into the dominant culture, whereas their parents inevitably struggle with ambivalence. While the parents actively support the acquisition of certain cultural competencies, they fight to ward off the corrupting influences of the new society.

Consider the case of a Ghanaian taxi driver in New York City whose two eldest sons are attending Brown and Duke. He hopes that his third son, in tenth grade, will be admitted to Harvard. He confided to us: "I make sure I know my children's friends and if they want to come to my house they have to follow my rules . . . And I never let my children work . . . Who knows what influences they will be exposed to at a job?"

In Dominican immigrant Julia Alvarez's hilarious novel *How the Garcia Girls Lost Their Accents,* she describes the struggle:

> We began to develop a taste for the American teenage life, and soon, Island was old hat, man . . . By the end of a couple of years away from home, we had *more* than adjusted.
>
> And of course, as soon as we had, Mami and Papi got all worried they were going to lose their girls to America. The next decision was obvious: we four girls would be sent summers to the Island so we wouldn't lose touch with *la familia.* The hidden agenda was marriage to homeland boys, since everyone knew that once a girl married an American, those grandbabies came out jabbering in English and thinking of the Island as a place to get a suntan.[3]

Immigrant parents walk a tightrope; they encourage their children to develop the competencies necessary to function in the new culture, all the while maintaining the traditions and (in many cases) language of home. Hence, children are encouraged to learn English, but at the same time may be asked to keep the new language and cultural ways out of the home. If they do not do so, children may be accused of "becoming American." Immigrant parents may experience their increasingly Americanized children as disrespectful, or may accuse them of becoming "cold" or "less demonstrative."[4]

Certainly, many struggle to maintain the features of the "old culture" in part because traditions and cultural behaviors provide both internalized standards of behavior and a soothing sense of social safety. Culture provides us with models for understanding experience and for sorting out meanings. Cultural belief systems also provide what we term a "field of safety." Cultural "safety nets," including interpersonal networks and shared understandings, generate the support required to walk the human walk. These cultural safety nets are deeply undermined in the process of immigration; immigrants must attempt to walk a delicate line separating two cultural orders.

In all societies, a critical role of parents is to act as guides for their children. Immigration undermines this function by removing the "map of experience" necessary to competently escort the children in the new culture.[5] Without effortless proficiency in the new culture, immigrant parents are less able to provide guidance in negotiating the currents of a complex society; they must also rely on their children for cultural explanations. As a seasoned immigrant comments to a prospective migrant in E. Annie Proulx's novel *Accordion Crimes*, "the natural order of the world is reversed. The old learn from the children."[6] By insisting that "under our roof" all will continue as it was in the old country, immigrant parents may be seeking to compensate. Often quite unconsciously, they seek to demonstrate that they are indeed competent, at least in the ways of the idealized old country.

Immigrant parents are also frightened by many of the very same features of American adolescence that are bemoaned by American parents, teachers, and social scientists—the disrespect of authority, the devaluing of education, the glorification of violence, and so forth. Many immigrant parents perceive what psychologist Lawrence Steinberg concluded in his analysis of a study of 20,000 high school students in urban, suburban, and rural areas: "[For immigrants today,] becoming Americanized is detrimental to youngsters' achievement, and terrible for their overall mental health."[7]

While immigrant parents worry about the corrupting influence of the American peer group, adolescents are most frequently drawn to the seductions of the new culture. The children of immigrants desperately want to be accepted, as most people do, and what is new for them is often what is most desirable. They understand that in order to survive, they must develop competencies in the ways of the new world. Hence, the pull to assimilate is—and always has been—extremely strong.

The conventional wisdom has long been that immigrants can move from their marginal position only by assimilating as quickly as possible. Immigrants have long been urged to speak English with their children, to leave behind traditions, and to incorporate habits of mainstream Americans. Assimilation has been viewed as taking place along a continuum whereby recent arrivals gradually, and through the generations, become ever more Americanized.

The first generation of immigrants does not completely assimilate into the new culture. The linguistic and cultural hurdles are simply too high and too many. Nonetheless, in previous waves of immigration, with adequate opportunities, a certain amount of luck, and great effort, the second and third generations of immigrants—especially those who were white—largely "disappeared" into the mainstream culture. This pattern of assimilation has generally been one of upward mobility. As we noted earlier, however, though this model holds true for many new immigrants today, it does not for others. While some follow the "old" immigrant pattern, others seem to be joining an increasingly multicultural underclass.[8]

The reasons for this shift are varied. Certainly, the changing nature of the opportunity structure plays a fundamental role. So does the quality of the infrastructure, including schools and social services available to ease the transition. Race and color are important features differentiating this wave of immigration from earlier waves dominated by European origin populations. Enduring racial tensions and ethnic stereotypes are powerful constraints that all immigrants of color must contend with. But beyond these structural factors, what psychosocial processes are at play?

At no time in the lifespan is the urge to define oneself vis-à-vis the society at large as great as during adolescence. According to psychologist Erik Erikson, the single greatest developmental task of adolescence is to forge a coherent sense of identity.[9] For optimal development, Erikson argues that there needs to be a good fit between the individual's sense of self and the varied social milieus he or she must navigate. This model explained well the experiences of youth living in homogeneous worlds where there was significant complementarity across social spheres.

In an increasingly heterogeneous, transnational world, however, social spaces are more fractured and discontinuous than ever before. The Eriksonian theory of continuity and sameness in identity-making needs to be updated to effectively engage the complexities of experience in this era. Today, social scientists no longer consider identity a coherent, monolithic, and enduring construct.[10] Rather, new work struggles with an understanding of how identities are crafted and recrafted as youth make their way in varied social settings.

The experiences of the children of immigrants offer us a particularly powerful lens through which to view the workings of identity.[11] These children must construct identities that will enable them to thrive in profoundly different settings such as home, schools, the world of peers, and the world of work. Immigrant children today may have their breakfast conversation in Farsi, listen to African American rap with their peers on the way to school, and learn about the New Deal from their social studies teacher in mainstream English. When there is too much role confusion, when cultural guides are inadequate, and when there is cultural dissonance and strife, an adolescent will find it difficult to develop a flexible and adaptive sense of identity.

At the Margins

Immigrants are by definition in the margins of two cultures. Paradoxically, they can never truly belong either "here" nor "there." In

1937, E. V. Stonequist astutely described the experiences commonly involved in social dislocations. Cultural transitions, he argues, leave the migrant "on the margin of each [culture] but a member of neither."[12] An immigrant enters a new culture and no matter how hard she tries, will never completely belong; her accent will not be quite right, and her experiences will always be filtered through the dual frame of reference. Nor will she "belong" in her old country; her new experiences change her, altering the filters through which she views the world. Stonequist contends that marginality is intensified when there are sharp ethnic contrasts and hostility between the old and new cultures.

In addition to living in the cultural margins where old and new come together, immigrants must also navigate the complexities of the status system in the new country. Social systems are always stratified—whether by age, gender, division of labor, class, caste, or specialized sacred knowledge. In industrial societies, conflicts are often attributed to class dynamics and contradictions.[13] A person's work and educational levels determine much of his social experience. A defining feature of class systems is the idea of mobility; with sufficient effort (pursuit of education and hard work) and opportunities, a person can move up the social ladder. In societies such as India, however, another elaborate form of stratification—the caste system—rigidly separates groups and does not allow status mobility. By definition, caste systems rule out individual status mobility— once an Untouchable, forever an Untouchable.[14]

Status represents the building block of all stratification systems. In any social system, status slots are intertwined with role behaviors and expectations—those of the CEO, a manager, an assembly worker. Status defines and assigns role behaviors; these cultural scripts make social life more predictable through tacit shared expectations and behavioral repertoires. While making life predictable, status and role behaviors also structure inequalities in social interactions.

Immigrants enter the social hierarchy of the new society under a wide range of circumstances. While an upper-status professional immigrant may feel culturally marginal, she is likely to be able to enter the new society's status system at a more advantageous point than a poor and uneducated immigrant. In turn, the opportunities available to her children will be greater than those for children of immigrants entering the lower echelons of the status hierarchy.

In ethnically diverse and increasingly transnational societies, how does schooling relate to hierarchies of inequality?[15] Does the educational system reproduce inequalities by replicating the existing social order? Or does schooling help to overcome social inequalities by being an avenue for status mobility?

Cultural psychologist George De Vos and anthropologist John Ogbu have been at the forefront of theoretical work in the field of schooling and status inequality in ethnically complex societies.[16] Three themes dominate this body of scholarship. First, how do immigrant and minority groups enter the new society? Did they come as voluntary migrants or were they incorporated against their will through slavery or conquest? Second, do these groups face a structural ceiling above which they cannot rise in the status hierarchy regardless of motivation, talent, and achievement? Third, is the cultural and symbolic ethos of reception saturated with psychological disparagement and racist stereotypes? These three factors will have a profound relevance for any understanding of schooling experiences as well as for the identity formation of minority and immigrant children.

What is the experience of self in cultures where patterned inequality shapes social interactions? George De Vos and Marcelo Suárez-Orozco have developed an interdisciplinary psychocultural model to examine the experience of inequality in structural and psychological terms.[17] While all groups face structural obstacles, not all groups elicit and experience the same attitudes from a dominant culture. Social science research has demonstrated that some immigrant groups elicit more negative attitudes than others do. In U.S. public opinion polls, for example, Asians are seen more favorably than Latinos.[18]

In cases where racial and ethnic inequalities are highly structured, such as for Algerians in France, Koreans in Japan, or Mexicans in

California, "psychological disparagement" and "symbolic violence" dominate the immigrants' experience. Members of these groups not only are effectively locked out of the opportunity structure (through segregated and inferior schools, and through work opportunities limited to the least desirable sectors of the economy) but also commonly become victims of cultural violence. They are stereotyped as "innately inferior," "lazier," "prone to crime," and therefore less deserving of sharing in the dominant society's dream. Facing such charged attitudes that assault and undermine their sense of self, minority children may come to experience the institutions of the dominant society—and most specifically its schools—as alien terrain reproducing an order of inequality.[19]

Stanford University social psychologist Claude Steele has been at the forefront of new theoretical and empirical work on how "identity threats," based on group membership, can profoundly shape academic achievement. In a series of ingenious experimental studies, Steele and his colleagues have demonstrated that under the stress of a stereotype threat, performance goes down on a variety of academic tasks. He maintains that when negative stereotypes about one's group prevail, "members of these groups can fear being reduced to the stereotype."[20] He notes that in these situations, self-handicapping increases. This "threat in the air" has both an immediate effect on the specific situation that evokes the stereotype threat and a cumulative erosive effect when continual events that evoke the threat occur. He argues that the stereotype threat shapes both intellectual performance and intellectual identity.

Data from a variety of studies demonstrate that immigrant children enter the United States with very positive attitudes toward education.[21] But these attitudes cannot be maintained in a climate of insurmountable obstacles, cultural hostilities, identity threats, and psychological disparagement. Under such circumstances most children will not continue to invest in schools as a way of moving up socially. Indeed, when facing toxic levels of cultural violence, children will tend to spend much of their psychic energy defending against these assaults on their sense of self.

Social Mirroring

How do such charged attitudes and hostilities affect the immigrant child's sense of self? Are immigrant children aware of these hostilities? We asked immigrant children what the hardest thing about immigration was. Discrimination and racism were recurring themes discussed by many of the children—especially those of Caribbean and Latino origin. The following statements are representative of the responses we received. A fourteen-year-old Mexican boy told us: "The discrimination [is the hardest thing]. . . You see it in the streets and on TV, and you hear it on the radio." A thirteen-year-old Chinese girl responded: "Americans discriminate. They treat you badly because you are Chinese or black. I hate this most." "They treat immigrants like animals. There are a lot of racist people," reported a thirteen-year-old Mexican girl. Immigrant children experience discrimination in a variety of forms and settings. A fourteen-year-old Haitian girl said: "I do not like the discrimination. For example, when you go to a store, whites follow you to see if you are going to take something." A twelve-year-old Haitian boy told us: "There are many teachers that treat us [the students] well, but there are many who do not. There are teachers who even though they deny it, are racists." A fourteen-year-old Haitian boy summed it up by saying: "The racism is here. The Americans believe they are superior to other races."

We asked all the children in our study to complete the following sentence: "Most Americans think [people from my country] are ————." Haitian children were asked: "Most Americans think Haitians are ————"; Mexican children were asked: "Most Americans think Mexicans are ————," and so forth. Strikingly, for Latino and Haitian immigrants, the most common association was "Most Americans think that we are *bad*." Overwhelmingly, the children reported that Americans had negative perceptions about them. Below is a sample of responses we received:

> "Most Americans think that we are stupid." (ten-year-old Haitian girl)

"Most Americans think that we can't do the same things as them
in school or at work." (ten-year-old Mexican girl)
"Most Americans think that we are useless." (fourteen-year-old
Dominican girl)
"Most Americans think that we are garbage." (fourteen-year-old
Dominican boy)
"Most Americans think that we are members of gangs." (nine-
year-old Central American girl)
"Most Americans think that we are thieves." (thirteen-year-old
Haitian girl)
"Most Americans think that we are lazy, gangsters, drug-addicts
that only come to take their jobs away." (fourteen-year-old
Mexican boy)
"Most Americans think that we are bad like all Latinos." (twelve-
year-old Central American boy)
"Most Americans think that we don't exist." (twelve-year-old
Mexican boy)

Fully 65 percent of our participants had a negative association to
the sentence "Most Americans think [people from the child's country of origin—Chinese/Dominicans/Central Americans/Haitians/
Mexicans] are ———." Furthermore, there were significant differences between groups. Of the Haitian and Dominican children, 80
percent or more gave negative responses, while the Chinese were the
least likely to give a negative response and the most likely to give a
neutral response (Table 4.1).

Table 4.1 Responses to the sentence completion task "Most people think
[people from my country] are ———"

Ethnic group	Negative	Neutral	Positive	Mixed
Chinese	47%	32.0%	19.0%	2%
Dominican	82%	8.5%	8.5%	1%
Central American	64%	8.0%	19.0%	9%
Haitian	80%	14.0%	6.0%	0%
Mexican	75%	8.0%	17.0%	0%

Source: Harvard Longitudinal Immigrant Student Adaptation study.

Over time, immigrant children develop a keen eye for discerning the place of race and color in the U.S. status hierarchy. A nine-year-old Dominican boy noted: In the United States "life is good to you if you are pretty and if you are white. If your face looks white and you are not very dark, life is good." A fifteen-year-old Chinese girl shared this with us: "I have many friends from Russia. They can fit in with the Americans well and easily participate in the society because their appearance is relatively similar to Americans. If they speak English without an accent, you can't tell that they are from another country. If others think you are American, they won't treat you differently. But Asians can be distinguished from the Americans very easily. I have a Chinese-American friend who was born here. But teachers always ask her 'Where are you from?'" Immigrant children of color know that many in the dominant culture do not like them or welcome them. Psychologically, what do children do with this reception? Are these attitudes of the host culture internalized, denied, or resisted?

Child psychoanalyst D. W. Winnicott suggests that the child's sense of self is profoundly shaped by the reflections mirrored back to her by significant others.[22] Indeed all human beings are dependent upon such reflections; "others" include not just the mother (Winnicott's focus), but also nonparental relatives, adult caretakers, siblings, teachers, peers, employers, people on the street, and even the media. When the reflected image is generally positive, the individual (adult or child) will be able to feel that she is worthwhile and competent. When the reflection is generally negative, it is extremely difficult to maintain an unblemished sense of self-worth.

These reflections can be accurate or inaccurate.[23] In some cases, the reflection can be a positive distortion. In such a situation the response to the individual may be out of proportion to his actual contribution or achievements. In the most benign case, positive expectations can be an asset.[24] In a classic study demonstrating the strength of the "self-fulfilling prophecy," when teachers believed that certain children were brighter than others (based on the experimenter randomly assigning some children that designation, unsubstantiated in fact), they treated the children more positively and assigned them higher grades. It is possible that some immigrant students, such as Asians, benefit somewhat from positive expectations of their competence as a result of being members of a "model minority"—though this label no doubt has its costs.[25]

We are more concerned, however, with negative distortions. What happens to children who receive mirroring on the societal level that is predominantly negative and hostile? Such is the case with many immigrant and minority children. W. E. B. Du Bois beautifully articulated this challenge of what he termed "double-consciousness"—a "sense of always looking at one's self through the eyes of others, of measuring one's soul by the tape of a world that looks on in . . . contempt and pity."[26]

Philosopher Charles Taylor notes: "our identity is partly shaped by recognition or its absence, often by the misrecognition of others, and so a person or group of people can suffer real damage, real distortion, if the people or society around them mirror back to them a confining or demeaning or contemptible picture of themselves. Nonrecognition or misrecognition can inflict harm, can be a form of oppression, imprisoning someone in a false, distorted, and reduced mode of being."[27] When the expectations are of sloth, irresponsibility, low intelligence, and even danger, the outcome can be discouragement. When these reflections are received in a number of mirrors including the media, the classroom, and the street, the outcome can be psychological devastation.

Even when the parents provide positive mirroring, it often cannot compensate for the distorted reflections that children encounter in their daily lives. In some cases, the child believes that the immigrant parent is out of touch with reality. Even when the parents' opinions are considered valid, they may not be enough to counteract the intensity and frequency of the "house of mirrors" kind of distortions that immigrant children of color encounter in their everyday lives.

Esmeralda Santiago notes that although her mother had high expectations for her children, "outside of our door, the expectations were lower . . . [T]he rest of New York viewed us as dirty spicks, potential muggers, drug dealers, prostitutes." As a result she cultivated a comforting fantasy: "In my secret life, I wasn't Puerto Rican. I wasn't American. I wasn't anything. I spoke every language in the world so I was never confused about what people said and could be understood by everyone. My skin was no particular color, so I didn't stand out as black, white, or brown."[28]

Our data suggest that immigrant children are keenly aware of their reception. What can a child do with these hostilities? We have developed a conceptual model to examine the various ways that children of immigrants react to negative social mirroring. As illustrated in Figure 4.1, far from being predictably unilineal, we claim that the youth's responses are fluid and depend on a variety of factors—some social and some personal. Furthermore, the children of immigrants may change which of the various pathways highlighted in our model that they follow at different points in their development depending upon the circumstances in their lives—the neighborhoods they live in, the schools they attend, the relationships they develop, and the opportunities they encounter.

Some children will become resigned to the negative reflections. The hopelessness and self-deprecation that this resignation causes may in turn result in low aspirations and self-defeating behaviors. The general affect associated with this pathway is one of depression and passivity. In this scenario, the child is likely to respond with self-doubt and shame, setting low aspirations in a kind of self-fulfilling prophecy: "They are probably right. I'll never be able to do it."

Other youth mobilize to resist the mirrors and injustices they encounter. Here we differentiate between two types of resistance. The first is a project infused with hope, a sense of justice, and a faith in a better tomorrow. In the second case, youth may actively resist the reflections they encounter but are unable to maintain hope for change or a better future.[29] Without hope, the resulting anger and compensatory self-aggrandizement may lead to acting-out behaviors including the kinds of distopic cultural practices typically associated with gang membership. For these youth, the response is "You think I'm bad? Let me show you how bad I can be."

The social trajectories of youth who are actively able to maintain and cultivate a sense of hope for the future are more promising. Whether they are resigned, oblivious, or resistant to the reflections

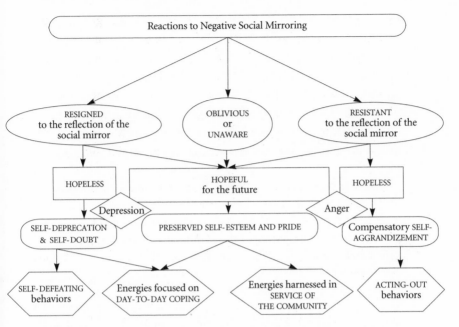

Figure 4.1 Reactions to negative social mirroring. Note that hope is essential for a positive outcome.

in the social mirror, those who are able to maintain hope are in fundamental ways partially inoculated to the negative mirroring that they encounter. These youth are better able to maintain a sense of pride and healthy self-esteem. In these circumstances, their energies are freed up and mobilized for the work of day-to-day coping. Some may not only focus on their own advancement but also serve their communities by volunteering to help others, acting as role models, or advocating and working for social change. In this scenario, youth respond to the negative social mirror with "I'll show you. I'll make it in spite of what you think of me."

Crafting Identities

Cultural dislocation and social mirroring greatly influence the remaking of the immigrant's identity. Immigrant and minority youth will pick up powerful cues from the social environment about what is expected of them. Ruben Navarette, Jr., a fully Americanized grandson of a Mexican immigrant, reflects upon the force of such cultural expectations in the patterning of identity. He describes his voyage from a predominantly Mexican American town in California's Central Valley to Harvard University. This voyage, a counter-migration of sorts, signifies above all a change in social personae.[30] It is a story filled with poignant paradoxes. Navarette goes from being "culturally white" in a Mexican town to becoming "Mexican" at New England's white bastion. Navarette describes his initial feelings:

> It begins appropriately, as it does with students of all color, with a distinct element of self-doubt. For generations, bright young adults have wandered through Harvard Square in the first few weeks feeling like frauds. We are convinced that the admissions officer must have made some dreadful mistake. This is Harvard, we tell ourselves . . . What are we doing here?
>
> For Latinos, and other minority students who may see themselves—indeed, have been encouraged by hometown insults to see themselves—as the winners of the dubious affirmative action lottery, the question of unworthiness endures like a stale odor. You begin to believe old critics, assuming that you have come to this bizarre place not by your own merit but by the grace of a government handout.[31]

Navarette senses an "implied expectation that I serve as a cultural ambassador to sheltered white people" (83). He describes his process of developing an ethnic persona, though he "remember[s] that, up to that point . . . I did not even really consider myself Mexican American" (76). In the process he develops "a new sense of illegitimacy . . . I felt that I was being asked to produce something that, at the time, I barely myself understood" (83).

He begins to question his ability to transmit a culture that he had only just recently embraced and was "not my culture, really, but my Mexican grandfathers'" (83). He admits to knowing first-hand more about hamburgers, Bruce Springsteen, CNN, and the Little League than of mole, Vincente Fernandez, Univisíon, and soccer. He then begins to fabricate and perform a new ethnic identity: "If I did not have culture then I would manufacture it. If I did not have a truly ethnic persona, then I would create one. I exaggerate my ethnicity" (69). While at Harvard he crafts a Mexican persona: "Resisting assimilation, I wanted to be noticed, seen as different. I wore my ethnicity as a badge. No, a shield. Like a Halloween costume" (69). Given his newly crafted persona, he struggles with feelings of being a "fraud . . . culturally impotent . . . and an ethnic impostor" (84). He struggles to understand who he is and whether there is anyone else quite like him.

Identities and Styles of Adaptation

Navarette's journey suggests that identities and styles of adaptation are powerfully linked to context and social mirroring. In some cases children of immigrants embrace total assimilation and complete identification with mainstream American culture. In other cases, a new ethnic identity is forged, one that incorporates selected aspects of both the culture of origin and mainstream American culture. In still other cases, an adversarial identity emerges. Each identity style influences the child's academic experience and his or her subsequent adaptation to the new society.

Even within the same family, each child may adopt his or her own way. The film *Mi Familia* (My family) portrays beautifully the ranges in identity formation and interpersonal styles in a group of siblings growing up in immigrant East Los Angeles. The identities they construct include an Anglo-oriented "Yuppie" attorney who is clearly embarrassed by his family's "Mexicanness," a gang member who battles it out with oppressive American authority figures, and a human rights activist who acquires many of the tools of the mainstream society to fight for the rights of immigrants and refugees.

ETHNIC FLIGHT

The children of immigrants who structure their identities around what we call an ethnic flight style most strongly identify with the dominant mainstream culture. These youth, like the "Yuppie" attorney in the film, may feel most comfortable "hanging out" and networking with peers from the mainstream culture rather than with their less acculturated peers. For these youth, learning to speak standard English is not only a way of communicating; it also becomes an important symbolic act of identifying with the dominant culture. Among these youth, success in school may be seen not only as a route for individualistic self-advancement, but also as a way to symbolically and psychologically move away from the world of the family and the ethnic group.

Often this identification with the mainstream culture results in a weakening of ties to members of their own ethnic group. These young people all too frequently are alienated from their less enculturated peers; they may have little in common with them or may even feel that they are somewhat superior. While they may gain entry into privileged positions within mainstream culture, they will still have to deal with issues of marginalization and exclusion.

Even when they do not feel superior to their ethnic peers, they may find these same ethnic peers unforgiving of any behaviors that could be interpreted as "ethnic betrayal." It is not necessary for the child of an immigrant to consciously distance himself from his culture. Among some ethnic groups, merely being a good student will result in sanctioning by peers. Accusations of "acting white," or of being a "coconut," a "banana" or an "Oreo" (brown, yellow, or black on the outside and white on the inside) are common.[32]

We contend that while ethnic flight is a form of adaptation that can help a person "make it" by the mainstream society's standards, it frequently comes at a significant social and emotional cost. Richard Rodriguez's autobiographical account of his experiences growing up in Sacramento, California, provides a rich illustration of an individual who attempts to integrate himself into the mainstream society by actively rejecting his native tongue, familial networks, and culture.[33] It also captures with poignancy how issues of shame and self-doubt are interwoven in situations of cultural dislocation, ethnic prejudice, and social mobility.

By the standards of mainstream society, Rodriguez is certainly successful. As a Stanford, Columbia, and Berkeley graduate and fellow of the prestigious Warbug Institute in London, he came a long way from the humble Sacramento barrio of his youth. But a close reading of his controversial autobiography reveals the poignant shame, marginality, and alienation that characterizes his journey.

Like many immigrant parents, Rodriguez's mother is stymied in her attempts to get ahead, so she "will[s] her ambition to her children. 'Get all the education you can. With an education you can do anything'" (54–55). His mother is told by the local nuns to stop using the family's "private" language (the language of intimacy—Spanish) and to start using the more instrumental "public" language (English) at home. Soon, Rodriguez admits to being "angry at them [his parents] for having encouraged me towards classroom English" (52). He found himself retaliating by intentionally hurting his parents, by correcting them when they made mistakes in English. "But gradually this anger was exhausted, replaced by guilt as school grew more and more attractive to me" (50).

The more that Rodriguez was propelled toward the "public" world of school and the mainstream culture, the more alienated he became from his "private world"—that of his family, ethnicity, and culture. This, in part, was fueled by his embarrassment about his parents' accent and their inability to help him with even second-grade homework. "Your parents must be proud of you . . . Shyly I would smile, never betraying my sense of irony: I was not proud of my mother and father" (52). Unable to identify with his parents, Rodriguez turns to his teachers. "I wanted to be like my teachers, to possess their knowledge, to assume their authority, their confidence, even to assume a teacher's persona" (55).

In acquiring English and an education, Rodriguez gained as well as lost. He gained both the capacity to enter the public arena he so much valued, as well as the ability to communicate and command the attention of powerful members of the dominant culture—indeed, he became their interpreter of "Mexican" and "immigration" issues in the media circuit. But he lost emotionally on several levels. Most important, he lost the feeling of belonging to his family. With the transition to English, his family was "no longer so close; no longer bound tight by the pleasing and troubling knowledge of our public separateness" (23). He lost the easy intimacy and open communication between family members. A numbness engulfs Rodriguez, separating him from his increasingly "foreign" parents. The child of Mexican migrants, he himself becomes a migrant leaving his family behind in his journey to "success."

Rodriguez's experience is constructed as a choice between instrumental mobility ("making it" in the world of the mainstream society) and expressive affiliation. Although he "makes it," Rodriguez is profoundly alone—alienated from his family and his peers, finding few who are able or willing to take his path. He then must rationalize his choice with the consequent gains as well as losses. In doing so, he becomes a vocal opponent of both bilingual education and affirmative action: he invokes the archaic—and narcissistic—assimilationist argument that because he "made it" by renouncing his ethnicity, so should others.

In reading Rodriguez, we are left with profound sadness for both him and his parents. He is so alone that the only sense of intimacy he seems to have is with his readers: "encouraged by physical isolation to reveal what is most personal; determined at the same time to have my words seen by strangers" (187). His parents lose a favorite son. The mother's attempts at intimacy and involvement are consistently rebuffed. The son's only apparent identification with his father is with his silence. The gulf between them seems interminable and irreparable.

Rodriguez's devastating account goes directly to the symbolic and affective aspects of both language and culture. To see language as a mere tool for communication is to miss its deep affective roots. By losing competency in the language of origin, the child of immigrants may also lose much of the sustenance that the culture of origin provides.

In an earlier era of scholarship, this style of adaptation was termed "passing."[34] While there were gains for the children of immigrants who "disappear" into the mainstream culture, there were also hidden costs—primarily in terms of unresolved shame, doubt, and self-hatred. While "passing" may have been a common style of adaptation among those who looked like the mainstream, it is not easily available to today's immigrants of color who visibly look like the "other."

ADVERSARIAL IDENTITIES

In the case of ethnic flight, children of immigrants mimic and identify with the dominant culture. At the opposite end of the continuum, some children of immigrants develop an adversarial stance toward the mainstream. These children construct identities around rejecting—after having been rejected by—the institutions of the dominant culture.

Princeton sociologist Alejandro Portes observes, "As second generation youth find their aspirations for wealth and social status blocked, they may join native minorities in the inner-city, adopting an adversarial stance toward middle-class white society, and adding to the present urban pathologies."[35] Immigrant children who find themselves structurally marginalized and culturally disparaged are more likely to respond to these challenges to their identities by developing an adversarial style of adaptation. These children of immigrants are responding in similar ways to that of other marginalized youth in the United States—such as many inner-city poor African Americans or Puerto Ricans (and elsewhere such as Koreans in Japan or Algerians in France). Likewise, following previous waves of immigration, many of the disparaged and disenfranchised second-generation Italian American, Irish American, and Polish American adolescents fit a similar profile.

Today some children of immigrants, including Latino, African, Caribbean, and Asian youth, also respond to marginalization and the poisoned mirror by developing adversarial identities. Like other disenfranchised youth, children of immigrants who develop adversarial identities tend to have problems in school and are more likely to drop out, and consequently face unemployment in the formal economy. Those drawn to the periphery—and epicenter—of gangs are also disproportionally represented in the penal system.

Among children of immigrants who gravitate toward adversarial styles, embracing aspects of the dominant culture is equated with giving up one's own ethnic identity.[36] Among youth engaged in adversarial styles, speaking standard English and doing well in school may be interpreted as a show of hauteur and as a wish to "act white." Navarette recalls the taunts from his less successful peers, "They will

call me 'Brain' as I walk through hallways in the junior high school
. . . They will accuse me, by virtue of my academic success, of 'trying
to be white.'"[37] When adolescents acquire the idea that doing well
in school is an act of ethnic betrayal, it becomes problematic for
them to develop the behaviors and attitudes necessary to succeed in
school. Adversarial styles quite severely compromise the future opportunities of children who are already at risk of school failure because of poverty, inequality, and race.

In his novel *Pocho*, José Villareal poignantly articulates the effects
of cultural marginality and the poisoned mirror on the children of
Mexican immigrant workers. In this passage, Villareal's protagonist
describes how racism and disparagement shape the adversarial cultural styles of the second generation:

> They had a burning contempt for people of different ancestry, whom
> they called Americans, and a marked hauteur towards Mexico and to-
> ward their parents for their old-country ways. The former feeling
> came from a sense of inferiority that is a prominent characteristic in
> any Mexican reared in southern California; and the latter was an in-
> explicable compensation for that feeling. They needed to feel superior
> to something, which is a natural thing. The result was that they at-
> tempted to segregate themselves from both their cultures, and be-
> came truly a lost race . . . [I]n spite of their behavior, which was sen-
> sational at times and violent at others, they were simply a portion of
> confused humanity, employing their self-segregation as a means of
> expression.[38]

Those children of immigrants who are not able to embrace their
own culture and who have formulated their identities around rejecting aspects of the mainstream society may be drawn to gangs. For
such youth, who lack meaningful opportunities, gangs offer a sense
of belonging, solidarity, protection, support, discipline, and warmth.
Gangs also structure the anger many feel toward the society that vio-
lently rejected their parents and themselves. Although many second-
generation youth may look to gangs for cues about dress, language,
and attitude, most remain on the periphery and eventually outgrow
the gang mystique after working through the identity issues of ado-

lescence. The gang ethos provides a sense of identity and cohesion for marginal youth during a turbulent stage of development.[39]

Urban anthropologist Diego Vigil explores several factors in the development of Latino and Asian immigrant gangs. These include urban poverty and limited economic opportunity, ethnic minority status and discrimination, lack of training and education, and a breakdown in the social institutions of school and family. Vigil points out that for Mexican immigrants, gangs have been a long-lasting rather than transitory phenomenon—like gangs among earlier Italian and Irish immigrants. This is due to a unique situation of continuous migration from Mexico, which reproduces new cycles of marginality where more established members recruit newer arrivals in a seemingly uninterrupted cycle of gang initiation.[40]

The youth most drawn to gangs tend to have troubled backgrounds. They most often come from families that are poor, have absent or unavailable parents, are abusive, or have substance abuse problems. A common denominator seems to be the absence of strong figures such as parents, uncles and aunts, or older siblings who can help the youth navigate the tensions of adolescence. Without this strong support and guidance, these youth will turn for emotional support to those sharing their predicament—their peers.

A perceptive teacher told us, "The gangs are in their community, in their own barrios. They see the gangs all around them. Their parents are often gone all day at work. So these kids are alone with no supervision. The parents are not there. The gangs offer company, it gives them protection. It is kind of a family. It is cool and exciting for them to belong to a gang." Another experienced teacher said: "These kids are in a desert. The gangs offer them company and protection. There is a pressure to join."

Luís J. Rodríguez's gripping, thinly disguised autobiographical novel of his gang involvement in East Los Angeles provides a powerful description not only of "this enigma of a boy, who looked like he could choke the life out of you one minute and then recite a poem in another" but also of many other children of immigrants who come to develop an adversarial identity.[41]

His immigration journey begins with a "first exposure in America [that] stays with me like a foul odor. It seemed a strange world, most of it spiteful to us, spitting and stepping on us, coughing us up, us immigrants, as if we were phlegm stuck in the throat of this country" (19). He recalls an incident when his mother sat her family down at an empty park bench. Soon, an American woman walks by and yells: "Look spic, you can't sit there! . . . You don't belong here! Understand! This is not your country!" (19). He reports feeling as though "we were invisible people in a city which thrived on glitter, big screens and big names, but this glamour contained none of our names, none of our faces. The refrain 'this is not your country' echoed for a lifetime" (19–20).

When he left Mexico for political reasons, Luís's father lost much of his social status. "This former teacher and biologist, who once labeled all the trees and plants in the backyard so we would know their scientific names" (113), now worked as a laboratory technician where he was nothing more than "an overblown janitor" (135). While Luís's father "was proud of what he did" (135), Luís felt deep shame. "My dad looked like a lowly peasant, a man with a hat in his hand—apologetic. At home he was king, *el jefito*—the 'word.' But here my father turned into somebody else's push-around. Dad should have been equals with anyone, but with such bad English . . . *Oh my father, why don't you stand up to them? Why don't you be the man you are at home?*" (136).

Although Luís's parents are physically present in his life, their authority is weakened by the shame Luís feels toward them. Their attempts to place limits on his acting-out behaviors are largely ineffective. By age thirteen, he was "Already tattooed. Already sexually involved. Already into drugs. In the middle of the night I snuck out through the window" (48).

Luís's family lived in a poor barrio in the "Hills." There they find that "for the most part, the Mexicans in and around Los Angeles were economically and socially closest to blacks" (84). The Mexican immigrants begin to master black English and "imitated the Southside swagger and style," and blacks adopted Mexican slang and some elements of the *cholo* style. Despite these interchanges, "this didn't mean at times we didn't war with one another, such being the state of affairs at the bottom" (84–85).

Luís attends a high school where "friction filled the hallways" (83). He astutely describes the class divisions and tracking in this setting:

> The school had two principal languages. Two skin tones and two cultures. It revolved around class differences . . . The teachers and administrators were overwhelmingly Anglo and whether they were aware of it or not, they favored the white students.
>
> If you came from the Hills, you were labeled from the start. I'd walk into the counselor's office for whatever reason, and looks of disdain greeted me—one meant for a criminal, an alien to be feared. Already a thug. It was harder to defy this expectation than to just accept it and fall into the trappings. It was a jacket that I could try to take off, but they kept putting it back on. The first hint of trouble and the preconceptions proved true. So why not be proud? Why not be an outlaw? Why not make it our own? (84–84)

With ineffectual parents and adults in school who expect the worst of him, Luís, like too many other disaffected youth, turned to his peers. They formed clubs or *clicas,* most of which

> began quite innocently. Maybe they were a team of guys for friendly football. Sometimes they were set up for trips to the beach or the mountains. But some became more organized. They obtained jackets, with their own colors and identification cards. Later a few of the clicas became car clubs who invested what little they had in bouncing low riders, street-wise "shorts," splashed with colors which cruised the main drags of local barrios or the main cruising spot we called the *boulevard.*
>
> Then also, some of the clubs metamorphosed into something more unpredictable, more encompassing. Something more deadly. (43)

Members of the *clica* would all take a pledge. They would be told by an older club member that the pledge was "to be for each other. To stand up for the *clica.* [It] will never let you down. Don't ever let [it] down" (41). These *clicas* provided solidarity, protection, and most seductively, an illusion of power: "I had yearnings at the time, which a lot of us had, to acquire authority in our lives in the face of police, joblessness and powerlessness (113).

Despite his reservations about violence, Luís fantasized about the power he would derive from his gang involvement: "I wanted this power. I wanted to be able to bring the whole school to its knees and even make teachers squirm. All my school life until then had been poised against me: telling me what to be, what to say, how to say it. I was a broken boy, shy and fearful. I wanted what [the *clica*] had; I wanted the power to hurt somebody" (42). But of course the price of all this is high: "We were constant prey, and the hunters soon become big blurs: the police, the gangs, the junkies . . . all smudged into one . . . We were always afraid. Always running" (36).

Luís eventually broke away from this lifestyle and in time became a successful author. He attributed his ability to break away to his love of books as well as an inspiring mentor. The "world of books" is his father's inheritance (139). Although he contended with his peers' teasing, he found inspiration and escape in reading. He also found in a local community center an older mentor whom he looked up to, someone who provided guidance and inspiration.

Luís Rodríguez's story captures a number of themes that we have found in the lives of many children of immigrants. They have been ostracized and humiliated by mainstream society; they have parents who are unable to guide them through the daunting obstacle course of adolescence; and they live in neighborhoods where there are no jobs and where gangs proliferate. They come to feel powerless and hopeless. During a vulnerable stage of development, gangs furnish the illusion of emotional, financial, and physical protection. Gangs appear to provide an initially exhilarating lifestyle—one that lies in sharp contrast to that provided by schools, which they view as not only uninspiring but also as rejecting them.

TRANSCULTURAL IDENTITIES

The large majority of children of immigrants develop an adaptational style between the extremes of "adversarial" and "ethnic flight." The work of immigration for these children is the crafting of bicultural identities. These youth must creatively fuse aspects of both cultures—the parental tradition and the new culture—in a process of transculturation that blends two systems that are at once their own and foreign. These children achieve bicultural and bilingual competencies that become an integral part of their sense of self. The culturally constructed social strictures and the authority of their immigrant parents and elders are seen as legitimate, while learning standard English and doing well in school are viewed as competencies that do not compromise their sense of who they are. These youth easily communicate and make friends with members of their own ethnic group as well as with students, teachers, employers, and colleagues of other backgrounds.

We have found that many who successfully "make it" clearly perceive and appreciate the sacrifices that loved ones have made to enable them to thrive in a new country. Rather than wishing to distance themselves from parents, these youth come to experience success as a way to "pay back" their parents for their sacrifices. At times, they experience a form of "survivor guilt" as a result of the deprivation that their parents and other family members have suffered in order to move to the new land. Among many such adolescents, success in school means not only self-advancement and independence, but also, and perhaps even more importantly, making the parental sacrifices worthwhile by "becoming a somebody." For such youth, "making it" may involve "giving back" to parents, siblings, peers, and other less fortunate members of the community.

We view the creation of transcultural identities as the most adaptive of the three styles. It preserves the affective ties of the home culture while enabling the child to acquire the skills required to cope successfully in the mainstream culture. This identity style not only serves the individual well, but also benefits the society at large. It is precisely such bicultural individuals whom Stonequist argued would be best suited to become the "creative agents" who might "contribute to the solution of the conflict of races and cultures."[42]

Seventeen-year-old Silvia in many ways typifies the transcultural style.[43] Silvia's goal is not to simply "Americanize," but rather to act as a bridge between her two very different worlds. She remains proud of her Latina heritage but eagerly pursues the cultural skills she deems necessary to "make it" in the new country. Silvia came to our attention when she organized a visit for other immigrant students to several local colleges in order to familiarize them with the educational opportunities in the area.

Silvia came to California in the wave of war and terror that swept Central America in the 1970s and 1980s. Her friends include students from a variety of backgrounds. She feels at ease with Anglo kids, as well as with Filipino, Chinese, and other Latino students. She switches back and forth between her native Spanish and her increasingly more sophisticated English.

Bound for one of the most prestigious universities in California, Silvia articulates the factors that have contributed to her highly successful career in an urban high school where the odds are stacked against the students. Silvia credits her family's recognition that higher education is needed to access the better opportunities in the United States; a cohesive family; a feeling of guilt over the sacrifices that her parents and other family members made to move them North; a charismatic teacher who took her under his wing; and her own hard work and optimism.

Silvia feels at ease shuttling back and forth between cultural boundaries. Her worldview is organized around comparing and contrasting experiences and opportunities in the two settings, her native El Salvador and her adopted United States. In talking about El Salvador, she speaks warmly of family, peers, and the ease of community life. But she notes that with the war in El Salvador, life had become dominated by fear, deprivation, nepotism, and rampant corruption. In the United States, although the social climate was "cold," it was also "a place where you could go up or you could go down."

She first became aware of opportunities for advancement while working part-time in Arizona, soon after arriving in the United States. There, while working for a janitorial service, she realized that whereas all the workers were monolingual Spanish speakers without much schooling, all of the supervisors were bilingual, "educated people." At that point, she said, "I realized that the way to make it in this country is with an education." Indeed, doing well in school is central to how Silvia thinks about opportunity in the new country. She also realizes that "to succeed in school, students need to have initiative, work hard, and be serious so that they can be taken seriously."

She credits an American high school psychology teacher with providing valuable cultural advice. She said,

> He would tell me "In this country, these are things you must do." And I would listen to him. He taught me not to be afraid of anyone. He said, "Don't be afraid of a gringa because she is better dressed than you are: we are all equal in this country. Don't be afraid to be different. In this country we are all different."
>
> . . . He changed me forever . . . He even found me a job, working as an intern with a councilman. I worked in his office. I had to quit that job because I needed a paid job. But I learned a lot there. I met a lot of people. I spoke English there and I slowly lost my fears.

Silvia immerses herself in the task of understanding how to succeed in the new society. From her American teachers, coworkers, and friends, she learns about mainstream cultural models of success. She has come to believe that in the United States, unlike in El Salvador, it is not adaptive to submit to authority. She learns that if an injustice occurs, the victim has rights and is expected to fight for them. If a counselor expects too little of a student and assigns them a noncollege preparatory class, the student is expected to request the change. If a teacher makes a disparaging remark to a student, that student can challenge it or at least know that regardless of who says it, such a comment is wrong. She is convinced that whereas "in Latin America, what matters is who you know, in the U.S. what matters is what you know."

She feels that too many Latino students believe that finishing high school is the pinnacle of success. She understands that what counts is to do well in the classes that prepare students for college: "I want to go to the university and my parents want me to go to the university. They do not want me to lead a life like the way they had to live when they were young. My parents had to work very hard, sacrifice themselves, and moving here was very hard. Everything was difficult and expensive. They suffered so that we could come here. Now what I want to do is to become a professional, to become a somebody, to work with my people here as a doctor."

Silvia devotes a great deal of time to helping other immigrant students. She tutors them in math and English and takes them to the library to find the books they need to complete their assignments. She talks to teachers about the problems her peers are facing, often recruiting friendly teachers to help students find jobs, to act as references, and to fill out papers for social service agencies. When she feels that a teacher or administrator is discriminating against a student, she advocates for her peers. She encourages fellow students to think beyond high school and urges them to change out of dead-end classes. She recounts how her friend Estella was afraid to ask a teacher to switch into a computer class. She encouraged Estella to talk to the teacher, coaching her to "tell her that if she helps you, you could do it. You see, I don't understand this fear. I cannot understand being afraid of talking to that person because that person is in a higher position. I know that person is in a higher position and I respect that. But I am not afraid. We are both human beings. The only difference is that she is now better educated than I am. But I can also become more educated."

Silvia felt that many other immigrant students who were not doing as well in school were operating with cultural models that did not work in their new environment. An important part of Silvia's identity was acting as a cultural broker between recent immigrants and "Americans."

> Studying is really the only way to help my community. I want to study and work. To see how to change things for the better in this *barrio*. I go out of this area into other districts, and I see how Americans live better than here. They have better houses, better schools, better jobs. Everything is better. And look at us here [she gestures around the

room]. Look at our neighborhood, with dealers coming up to you to sell drugs, with alcoholics living in the streets, and with prostitutes everywhere. So we come here, and many of us, rather than go up, we go down.

While Silvia is increasingly aware of discrimination and barriers to success, she is also keenly cognizant of the relative opportunities available to her and other immigrant children in the new country. The changes that immigration brings about, including the acquisition of new cultural competencies and social attitudes, is accompanied by a powerful sense of purpose where success becomes a way to give back to others including parents, siblings, and other members of her immigrant community.

Transcultural identities are most adaptive in this era of globalism and multiculturalism. By acquiring competencies that enable them to operate within more than one cultural code, immigrant youth are at an advantage. The unilinear assimilationist model that results in ethnic flight is no longer feasible because today's immigrants are not unambivalently invited to join the mainstream society. The rapid abandonment of the home culture implied in ethnic flight almost always results in the collapse of the parental voice of authority. Furthermore, lack of group connectedness results in anomie and alienation. The key to a successful adaptation involves acquiring competencies that are relevant to the global economy while maintaining the social networks and connectedness essential to the human condition. Those who are at ease in multiple social and cultural contexts will be most successful and will be able to achieve higher levels of maturity and happiness.

Context and agency are two sides of the same coin. In approaching the varieties of the immigrant experience, we need to pay attention to both sides. The "structures of opportunity" or conversely, "fields of endangerment" that many children face are fundamental for understanding the paths that they choose in the new setting. While much of the social science research on immigration has catalogued how structural opportunities and impediments shape the lives of immigrant children, their own agency is often neglected. Yet the story of today's immigrant children is not complete without reference to their consciousness and agency. The typologies we offer represent a framework for understanding the inner experience of self in context.

Structuring Ethnic Identity

In recent decades, the study of ethnic and racial identity has generated a lot of academic interest in a variety of social science disciplines—anthropology, psychology, sociology, political science, and even philosophy. One of the difficulties in studying ethnic identity is that it is conceptualized and defined differently by different social science disciplines as well as by individual researchers.[44] Broadly speaking, sociologists and anthropologists tend to focus on the social dimensions of ethnic identity while psychologists tend to examine personal, emotional meanings in the development and achievement of an ethnic identity.

In this context we use the term ethnic identity to refer to a feeling shared by individuals in a given group and based on a sense of common origin, common beliefs and values, common goals, and shared destiny.[45] Implied in this definition is the idea of cultural pluralism where dominant majorities and ethnic minorities live together in a single nation.[46]

Our conceptual framework suggests that individuals gravitating toward an ethnic-flight style of adaptation tend to cultivate links with the majority group while consciously (and unconsciously) distancing themselves from their co-ethnics. At the opposite end of the spectrum, individuals engaging in what we term adversarial styles of adaptation actively resist the norms, values, and expectations of the dominant group. In the middle, we find the vast majority of individuals who struggle to actively forge links between their ethnic group and the majority population. Through a process of transculturation, these individuals endeavor to create hybrid identities and cultural formations that transform the "old" ethnic culture and the "new" majority culture in creative ways.

Ethnicity is at once ascribed and achieved. Social theorist David Hayes-Bautista makes a distinction between "ethnic identification" and "ethnic identity." By "ethnic identity" he refers to the internal process by which a person comes to feel like a member of a specific ethnic group. By "ethnic identification" he means the social process wherein ethnic membership is ascribed to an individual based on a perceived set of traits.

There are two sources in the ascription of ethnic group membership: those made by co-ethnics ("you are a member of *our* group") and those made by the majority group ("you are a member of *that* group").[47] One's personal ethnic identity then is largely shaped by the socially constructed ethnic identification.[48]

While sociologists and anthropologists focus on group factors, psychologists typically study how individuals come to terms with their social identities. Psychologists argue that identity goes through a variety of permutations (especially during adolescence) as the person "tries on for size" different identity strategies. Some psychologists claim that all individuals move steadily from a stage of ethnic or "racial unawareness," to one of "exploration," to a final stage resulting in an "achieved" sense of ethnic or racial identity.[49] Others have pointed out that the process of racial and ethnic identity formation may be more accurately described as following a "spiral" (rather than linear) path. A person may progress from one stage to the next and then revisit a previous stage, this time with a somewhat different vantage point.[50]

In our framework, we do not place the three dominant identity styles of adaptation that we have identified in a unilinear developmental sequence from least to most mature (though we do view the transcultural strategy as the most functional in today's transnational and multicultural world).[51] Rather, we intend these to describe how identity is experienced for the children of immigrants. Individuals may find themselves fitting into different styles at different times in their lives.

It is always important to keep in mind that an ethnic (or racial) identity has greater or lesser salience depending upon context. For example, a graduate student told us: "In Hong Kong, I never thought of myself as Asian; in the U.S. I am reminded that I am Asian daily." Likewise, among African Americans in the United States, race is a (if not the) central feature of identity. When they visit Africa, however, being American becomes the central characteristic of their sense of self.[52]

What draws a youth into one identity style rather than another? A variety of complex psychological, social, cultural, and economic factors influence why the children of immigrants gravitate to a certain identity style (Figure 4.2). In our view, the social mirror is of paramount importance among immigrant youth of color entering our society. Many new arrivals encounter a highly distorted reflection. Harvard sociologist Mary Waters has done extensive research examining how these issues manifest themselves among West Indian immigrants and their children. Waters claims that in this "race conscious society a person becomes defined racially and identity is imposed upon them by outsiders."[53] She reports that her black immigrant informants are shocked by the level of racism they encounter. Though they arrive expecting structural obstacles (such as discrimination in finding housing, receiving promotions, and so forth), what they find most distressing is the level of both overt and covert prejudice and discrimination. By overt, blatant acts of prejudice and discrimination Waters means physical attacks, verbal insults, as well as intimidation by police. By covert discrimination she is referring to the more subtle forms of "daily hassles, indignities and 'bad vibes' that black people experience constantly in interactions with whites."[54] Tragically, she concludes, "The suspicion that any individual white might treat one badly because of skin color begins to shape every encounter between black and white. Interpersonal racism ultimately undermined the ability of blacks and whites to ever 'forget race.' The ghosts of past bad encounters influence current encounters. The immigrants learn to expect race to permeate every potential encounter with a white American."[55]

Waters reports that her West Indian informants often distance themselves from African Americans in an attempt to protect them-

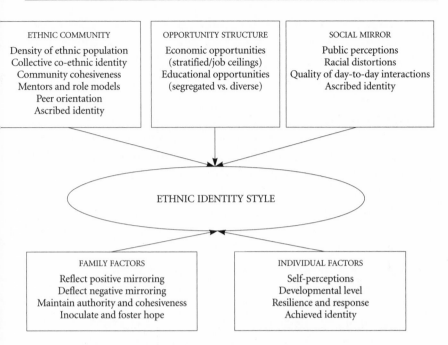

Figure 4.2   Factors influencing choice of ethnic identity style. We have found that for children of color, social mirroring has a strong effect.

selves from this emotionally toxic situation. This strategy has also been noted by researchers working with Haitian immigrants.[56] Flore Zéphir, a scholar of Haitian immigration, writes:

> Haitian immigrants bring with them their racial pride as part of the baggage from the motherland. However, when they disembark on the shores of America, they join a racially stratified society, and they are assigned a place at the bottom . . .
>
>   One of the first reactions of the Haitian immigrants against insulting social placement is to disaffiliate themselves with those placed in that category, namely native Blacks. By brandishing their nationality, they hope to accomplish many things. First, they expect an improved placement. Second, they want to send to Whites the message that they deserve to be treated differently because they are not American. Third, they want to maintain their positive Black identity, which

is tied to their national history. By constantly saying and reminding everyone that they are Haitian and nothing else, they seek to withstand any inferiority complex that the American system of categorization tries to give them.[57]

Mary Waters describes a number of characteristics that immigrants of color tend to bring with them that she speculates contribute to their relative success in the new setting. But she concludes that despite this combination of features, for their children, "Over the course of one generation the structural realities of American race relations and the American economy undermine the cultures of the West Indian immigrants and create responses among the immigrant, and especially their children, that resemble the cultural responses of African Americans to long histories of exclusion and discrimination."[58]

Immigrants who encounter a negative social mirror, structured inequality in the opportunity structure, as well as inferior schooling in violent and segregated neighborhoods, will face an arduous long-term struggle. In such cases, the issues faced by the immigrant generation are predictably quite different from those facing the second and subsequent generations. While the immigrant generation typically struggles to accommodate to inequities while maintaining hope, for all too many of their children hope is arguably the most tragic casualty of long-term racism and structured inequality.

Hope is the single trait that cuts across at least the initial stages of all immigrations. The hope for "a better tomorrow" is the mantra that almost all immigrants recite as they enter a new country. Hope is a critical characteristic that may well account for the slight advantage that immigrants have over successive generations. It is a quality that is likely to shift and fade as the children of immigrants, and the next generation in turn, encounter the structural limitations and ambivalent embrace of their new home. Many children of immigrants come to drink from the well of hope only to find it poisoned.

Other elements play a role in the alchemy of ethnic identity (trans)formation. They are embedded within the daily social worlds that surround and support the immigrant child—his or her family, school, peer group, and community. When the family and the community are able to provide love, supervision, ambition, role models, and hope, they can help inoculate the children from the distrust and hate that they are likely to encounter in the outside world.

Socioeconomic status plays an undeniable role; preexisting inequalities tend to intensify subsequent inequalities. Middle-class immigrants who arrive with more of what sociologists call "human capital" (education and resources) and "social capital" (networks and connections) will have an advantage in the struggle to protect and promote the welfare of their children. The neighborhoods and schools that parents can provide their children will play an important role in shaping their futures. That is the topic we turn to next.

5

THE CHILDREN OF
IMMIGRATION IN SCHOOL

Doing well in school is more important today than ever before. In this era of global economic restructuring, well-paid jobs that allow for advancement require education well beyond high school.[1] In particular, there is a widening gap between those working in the knowledge-intensive sectors of the economy and those working in the service sectors. In previous eras, well-paid manufacturing jobs allowed blue-collar workers, including immigrants, to achieve secure middle-class lifestyles without much formal education.[2] Those days are gone.

Completing and indeed going beyond a high school education is critical today and will be even more vital in the decades to come. The U.S. economy generates almost no meaningful jobs for high school dropouts; during the 1980s, the average real wage of high school dropouts fell by nearly 20 percent. Those with master's degrees or more, however, were able to keep up with inflation and achieve real gains in their wages. Formal schooling has become a high-stakes goal for the children of immigrants. For many of them, schooling is nearly the *only* ticket for a better tomorrow.

What are the attitudes about schooling and education of the children of immigrants upon arrival? How do these attitudes change over time? How do their prior experiences with schools in their country of origin influence their subsequent functioning in U.S. schools? And what role do immigrant parents play in the successful schooling of their children? Are schools preparing the children to face the challenges of an increasingly competitive global economy?

Love Is Not Enough

Immigrant parents and their children are very aware of the importance of education to their future success. We asked immigrant parents: "How do you get ahead in the United States?" and a reference to education was by far the most frequent response. A Dominican parent noted that the way to get ahead was by "studying, learning English, going to college, and becoming a professional." A Chinese parent eloquently told us: "The only way to do it is to do well in school . . . Knowledge is the most lasting thing. If you have an education you can have a more fulfilling life and nothing can defeat you. Material things are short-lived no matter how much you own. Only knowledge can last forever."

The parents' attitudes toward education are passed down to their children. The children of immigrants arrive in our schools with very positive attitudes toward teachers and other school authorities. In a study of adolescents of various backgrounds (Mexican immigrants, second-generation Mexican Americans, and a control group of non-immigrant, non-Latino whites), we asked our informants to respond "yes" or "no" to the statement: "In life, school is the most important thing." While only 40 percent of the non-Latino white students responded yes, 84 percent of the Mexican immigrant students did so.[3] Likewise, we asked all the children in our Longitudinal Immigrant Student Adaptation (LISA) study to respond "yes" or "no" to the statement "School is important to get ahead." Fully 98 percent of the children responded affirmatively. To the open-ended question "What do you like most about living here [in the United States]?" 44 percent of the children referred to their new school. Every child was asked to complete the sentence "School is ———." Of the children in our study, 72 percent completed the sentence with a positive association such as "my life," "my second family," "the pathway to success."

In addition to revealing positive attitudes in broad terms, immi-

Table 5.1   Responses to the sentence completion task "School is ———"

Ethnic group	Negative	Neutral	Positive
Chinese	2%	64%	34%
Dominican	0%	10%	90%
Central American	3%	19%	78%
Haitian	2%	23%	75%
Mexican	4%	14%	82%

Source: Harvard Longitudinal Immigrant Student Adaptation study.

grant children respect and appreciate their teachers and principals. Data collected in an earlier study suggest a similar picture.[4] We asked Mexican immigrant, second-generation Mexican-American, and non-immigrant white students attending the same school to complete the sentence: "My principal is ———." The immigrant adolescents had far more positive associations than did the other groups: 60 percent gave responses such as: "a good, capable person," "very friendly," "an exciting person." The two groups of U.S.-born children revealed more negative attitudes about the same principal. Only 28 percent of the white children had positive responses, while 40 percent revealed negative attitudes such as "a jerk," "an idiot," "a pain." The rest were neutral in their responses. The second-generation Mexican Americans fell between the two groups, with 32 percent having positive associations and another 32 percent having negative associations.

Are there group differences in incoming attitudes toward school and teachers? LISA data reveal an interesting pattern. Of the children in this study, 73 percent completed the sentence "Teachers are ———" with glowing attributes such as "a model to learn from," "good people," or "just like parents to us." But of all the groups, the Chinese children were the most likely to complete the sentence "School is ———" or "Teachers are ———." in a neutral way. They were more likely to give descriptive, neutral responses such as that school is "a place to learn" or "educational" and that teachers "are people who teach us" (Tables 5.1 and 5.2).

Many teachers who work closely with immigrant students delight in these positive attitudes. They go on at length about how their

Table 5.2 Responses to the sentence completion task "Teachers are ———"

Ethnic group	Negative	Neutral	Positive	Mixed
Chinese	4%	50%	42%	4%
Dominican	0%	7%	84%	9%
Central American	1%	10%	82%	7%
Haitian	0%	28%	69%	3%
Mexican	4%	7%	87%	2%

Source: Harvard Longitudinal Immigrant Student Adaptation study.

newly arrived students are better disciplined, more eager to learn, and more appreciative of their efforts than nonimmigrant students. One teacher comments, "These kids are bright. They learn better than American kids, they pay more attention, they care about learning." Another teacher told us, "Having those immigrant kids come here was the best thing that happened to this school." She went on to recount how racial tension had predominated in her school when the students were largely black or white. She added that once immigrant students arrived, "race ceased to be a big issue as the school became multiethnic instead of biracial."

Other teachers, however, are frustrated and reveal quite negative attitudes toward their newly arrived charges. These teachers seem to be responding to immigrants with the deep ambivalence found in the society at large. Some teachers view immigrant students as less intelligent, lazy, and more prone to get into trouble, and thus unlikely to assimilate into the mainstream. Some teachers made no attempt to censor such beliefs. One teacher said about her classroom of fifth-graders: "They give me kids with IQ's of 60 or 70 and they expect me to help them raise their grades. What am I, a miracle worker?" Another, talking about her class of middle-school immigrant students, predicted that one of her thirteen-year-old boys was going to "end up in jail" and that none "of my girls will go to college. They just don't have the IQ's." A superintendent of one of the largest school districts in the country said that his biggest concern was convincing his teachers and principals that immigrant and racial minority children were "teachable." His second biggest challenge was the budget.[5]

Teacher and student attitudes are only part of the larger story. The kind of love and reverence of school that immigrant children demonstrate may not always be enough to outweigh the multiple challenges and obstacles they typically encounter. What are these challenges?

Origins

Immigrant children arrive at American schools today from very different backgrounds that defy easy generalizations. On one end of the spectrum, we find children from middle-class urban backgrounds who have been preparing in their countries since early childhood for high-stakes, competitive exams. These children are typically highly literate and have well-developed study skills; their parents have taught them well what it takes to succeed in school. In sharp contrast are those children arriving from strife-ridden countries with little or no schooling. These children have missed critical years of classroom experience and often cannot read or write in their own language. They have not mastered the basics of either rote learning or the use of higher-level cognitive strategies. Classrooms suited for children their age may not meet their learning needs. Clearly, a child's educational experiences before coming to the United States will have a profound influence on his or her transition to American schools.

The varied socioeconomic and educational backgrounds of immigrant families will affect the child's opportunities and experiences in different ways. Parents with more resources can settle in more affluent and integrated neighborhoods that typically offer better schools for their children. Conversely, parents of more limited means will tend to gravitate to poorer neighborhoods where they are likely to find inferior schools. Highly educated parents are also better equipped to guide their children in how to study, structure an essay, and access information for school projects; they may also provide resources such as additional books, a home computer, and even tutors. More educated parents typically are in a better position to navigate the intricacies of the new school system. These parents are more likely to know the right questions to ask and will insist that their children be placed in educational programs that will ensure viable options in the future. They will know that not all courses are the same and indeed that not all schools produce the same outcomes.

The family's life before entering the United States also has an effect on school performance. Children fleeing strife and trauma come burdened with special needs. Many will need counseling for their psychological wounds before they can be ready to fully concentrate on their schoolwork.

Having the correct legal documents is also important for easing the transition to the American classroom. We have already noted that documented status can influence trust in school authorities, as well as access to the postsecondary educational system. Fear is a common theme in the schooling experiences of undocumented students. A high school student from Mexico tells of an incident soon after arrival: "At school the first week I was stopped in the hall and asked to see my green slip. I thought he meant my green card (immigration papers) and my heart raced. I was so scared I couldn't answer and was sent to the principal's office. It turned out he meant a slip from the teacher saying I had permission to be in the hall. I was afraid to tell the principal why I hadn't answered, so I lied."[6] Another high school student from Mexico shares the anxieties of many: "I don't have immigration papers . . . [T]he main thing is being afraid. All I want is my family to stay together and not have problems with the Migra [INS] . . . My teacher asks for my mother to sign a paper, but I am afraid to have her name in the school file. I am afraid they will deport her."[7]

In addition, not having the right schooling and vaccination records on hand affects the child's ability to enter the school system. In the course of our research, we encountered a number of cases where children were kept out of school months at a time because they lacked the papers from their country of origin needed to enroll. Even after the children enter the U.S. school system, keeping school records current and complete is often a continuing problem. As immigrant families move from one district to another in search of appropriate housing and better jobs, school records are often lost, misplaced, or not forwarded properly.

The New Neighborhoods

Contrary to widespread belief, immigrants today are overwhelmingly an urban population. Indeed, most immigrants tend to settle in our largest urban centers such as New York, Los Angeles, Chicago, Miami, and Houston. Some immigrants, however, are bypassing these large urban centers and settling in more racially integrated suburban neighborhoods. Newly arrived Latino and Caribbean immigrants follow a somewhat different path in settling than newly arrived Asian immigrants. Latino-origin neighborhoods have become increasingly more segregated in recent years, and new Latino immigrants tend to move to these neighborhoods. On the other hand, Asian immigrants often settle in more integrated neighborhoods and tend to enroll their children in schools that are predominantly white.[8]

Immigrants' choice of neighborhood in the United States will have important consequences for their interpersonal lives, experiences, and opportunities. In general, relationships play a decisive role in where immigrants settle. Florence, one of our informants, moved into a predominantly Haitian neighborhood, part of a larger African American neighborhood in the Mattapan district of Boston, because her aunt and uncle (who had migrated there earlier) found housing for her family nearby. The availability of affordable housing often determines where immigrants will settle.[9] For poor immigrants, "affordable" housing is often located in highly segregated neighborhoods where poverty prevails.

The neighborhood shapes the lives of immigrant children in many ways. The degree of racial segregation will have a series of important consequences. New arrivals of color who settle in predominantly minority neighborhoods will have virtually no direct contact with middle-class white Americans. This in turn will affect the kinds of English that the children will be exposed to, the networks that are available to access desirable jobs, and the quality of schools they attend.[10]

Concentrated poverty is associated with the "disappearance of meaningful work opportunities."[11] Adolescents in such neighborhoods are chronically underemployed or unemployed and must search for work elsewhere. In such neighborhoods with few opportunities in the formal economy, underground or informal activities tend to flourish. These kinds of economies often involve the trade of illegal substances and are associated with gangs and neighborhood violence.

When poverty is combined with racial segregation, the outcomes can be devastating. A large-scale sociological study concluded, "No matter what their personal traits or characteristics, people who grow up and live in environments of concentrated poverty and racial isolation are more likely to become teenage mothers, drop out of school, achieve only low levels of education, and earn lower adult incomes."[12]

Although deep neighborhood poverty and intense racial segregation are critical predictors of future outcomes, other factors play a role. George De Vos has argued that culturally constituted patterns of community cohesion and supervision can "immunize" immigrant youth from the more toxic elements in their new settings.[13] Likewise, Harvard Medical School psychiatrist Felton Earls and his colleagues have studied patterns of social cohesion in poor and segregated neighborhoods in Chicago. This research suggests that when communities are cohesive and when adults within the community can monitor youngsters' activities, the children tend to do better. Children that live in such communities are less likely to be involved with gangs and delinquency and are more focused on their academic pursuits.[14] Min Zhou has examined how community-based organizations geared to youth can make a tremendous difference in the life chances and opportunities of immigrant children.[15]

The immigrants' point of entry will shape their perceptions and opportunities in the new land. Middle-class immigrants who are able to join more integrated and more affluent communities will come to experience a very different America than those who settle among other immigrants or among native-born racial and ethnic minorities. They will be better able to maximize the opportunities that led them to migrate in the first place.

School Factors

Many neighborhood characteristics are reflected in the schools. How do these factors play out in schools? What are these schools like?

When an ethnographer enters a school, the thing that impresses her most, beyond its physical appearance and neighborhood context, is its social climate or ethos. This quality is often difficult to measure, but it is an essential factor in the everyday experience of schooling. The gifted ethnographer will pay attention to the following issues: Is there a charismatic leader at the helm? Does she project an aura of authority, and does she broadcast the expectation that all children, including immigrant children and other children of color, can learn and excel? Is morale among teachers and staff high or is the atmosphere one of suspicion, conflict, and tension? What is the nature of the relationship between teachers and students? Is it one of appreciation and mutual trust, or do teachers feel burdened and resentful of their new students? Does the school district provide teachers with adequate curriculum and training, as well as books and other supplies? What is the relationship between students of various backgrounds?

Research has demonstrated that effective schools have a number of common characteristics. These include: positive leadership and high staff morale; high academic expectations for all students regardless of background; a high value placed on the students' cultures and languages; and a safe and orderly school environment. Schools participating in the LISA project, which exemplify schools that immigrant children typically encounter, range from high-functioning schools with a strong culture of high expectations and a focus on achievement to catastrophic institutions characterized by ever-present fear of violence, distrust, low expectation, and institutional anomie.[16]

On the healthy end of the spectrum, we have identified schools that create "fields of opportunity" for immigrant students. In one such school located in a lower-middle-class integrated neighborhood in the outskirts of Boston, the campus, while not opulent, is well-kept and welcoming. Signs in multiple languages greet visitors, and student art and special projects decorate the walls. The computer lab is equipped with fairly up-to-date computers and software that the children frequently use. In this school, the principal's voice is strong, caring, and warm. A charismatic school counselor who is herself a Chinese immigrant knows in intimate detail the circumstances of each of her wards. Most teachers have advanced degrees in the subjects they are teaching. When we made a presentation about immigration, the room was crowded with interested and engaged teachers eager to learn more about the topic to better serve their immigrant students. We had planned a one-hour presentation, but the teachers kept us an additional hour with questions and comments.

Unfortunately, many other schools in our project (which represent the kinds of schools that many immigrant students attend) fall at the opposite end of the spectrum. Such schools are "fields of endangerment" where concerns with survival, not learning, prevail. Many such schools are located in neighborhoods troubled by drugs, prostitution, and gangs. At one school, one of our research assistants found that boys sneak out at noon to watch pornographic films at a convenience store nearby. Many of these schools are dilapidated and unkempt. In one, we were stunned to be met by a principal—obviously drunk at ten in the morning—who proudly proclaimed that five of her teachers had just requested a transfer. In some schools, violence is pervasive. In an elementary school participating in our study, a young girl was found raped and murdered on school premises. In a participating district, an irate parent stabbed a teacher in front of her students. In another school, just days after the Columbine incident, a cherry bomb was set off as one of our research assistants was conducting an interview. In many schools there is tremendous ethnic tension. At one of our sites, students regularly play a game called "Rice and Beans" (Asian students versus Latino students) that frequently deteriorates into physical violence. In many sites students report living in constant fear; they dread lunch and class changes because the hallways are places of confrontation and intimidation, including sexual violence. All too many schools have such "cultures of violence."[17]

These schools affect the opportunities and experiences of their many immigrant students in several immediate ways. They tend to have limited resources. School buildings are often poorly maintained and run down, and classrooms are typically overcrowded. Textbooks and curriculum are outdated; computers are few and obsolete. Many of the teachers may not have credentials in the subjects they teach. Clearly defined tracks sentence students to noncollege destinations. Because they lack strong English skills, immigrant students are often enrolled in the least demanding and least competitive classes, a path that eventually excludes them from courses needed for college. These schools generally offer few (if any) Advanced Placement courses, which are critical for entry in many of the more competitive colleges. The ratio of guidance counselors to students is impossibly low. Because the settings are so undesirable, teachers and principals routinely transfer out in search of better assignments elsewhere. As a result, in many such schools there is little continuity or sense of community. In these schools children and teachers are often preoccupied with ever-present violence and morale is often very low.

SEGREGATION IN SCHOOLS

Poverty and segregation are all too often highly correlated. A large-scale study by Harvard University scholars Gary Orfield and John Yun has found that among Latino immigrants, segregation has increased rapidly over the last two decades. This explains in large part why "Latino students have by far the highest drop-out rates of any major group in American schools and are experiencing declining access to college."[18] Asian students are generally more likely to enroll in integrated and relatively more affluent schools, which produce better results for their students.

It would be a mistake, however, to conclude that all Asian students are thriving in well-functioning integrated schools. The recent Asian immigrant student experience suggests two distinct path-ways.[19] As more Asian immigrants find themselves in poor and segregated schools, they face the same limited opportunities of other immigrants of color. As a result, for these students academic achievement and the pursuit of the American dream is more elusive. Orfield and his associates have found a dramatic range in academic performance among Chinese-origin immigrant students in San Francisco. While some are following the expectations attached to the "model minority" stereotype, others are struggling with schoolwork and are performing at the same level as other ethnic and racial minority students.[20]

BILINGUAL EDUCATION

A discussion of the experiences of immigrant children would not be complete without reference to the ever-controversial subject of bilingualism and bilingual education. Indeed, no topic related to immigration is as emotional and subject to political passion and manipulation than this issue. Why is this so? What are the realities of bilingual education? Are immigrant children learning English? Are they isolated in "linguistic ghettos" that doom them to second-rate citizenship?

That language should be the topic of emotional and politicized debate should not surprise anyone. While on the surface language is about communication, it is also a marker of identity and an instrument of power. The United States is not alone in experiencing tensions regarding bilingualism and second-language policy. While some countries such as Switzerland have worked out successful multilingual arrangements, other countries continue to struggle with this issue.

As a rule, where there are language-marked social inequities, the groups involved will resist (both consciously and unconsciously) mastering and using the other's language. Some proud Flemish speakers in Brussels simply refuse to speak in French (the once dominant language) in many social situations. Where one language is clearly a higher-status language, native speakers of the lower-status language often have trouble mastering and will indeed resist using the higher-status language. And native speakers of the high-status language seldom bother to use the second language.

In the United States, the controversies surrounding the teaching of a second language in schools suggest a number of paradoxes. While many view the mastery of a second or third language to be a clear advantage in this era of global capitalism and transnationalism, the public has deep reservations about teaching immigrant children in their native languages. Rather than being viewed as a potential asset to be cultivated, the linguistic skills brought by newly arrived immigrants are seen by many as a threat to the integrity of the English language and as a symbolic refusal to accommodate to American culture.

The debate over bilingualism in the United States is as old as the history of immigration itself. For example, in an earlier era of immigration, there were deep anxieties about the supposed threat that German-speaking immigrants posed to the English language. Even earlier, Benjamin Franklin vocally opposed teaching German on U.S. soil, fearing that Germans would never learn English and would thus fail to become loyal Americans.

German speakers were not alone. Many major immigrant groups to the United States—including Eastern Europeans, Chinese, and Japanese—eventually organized their own after-school language programs. These programs were developed to teach the children of immigrants in their own languages about their cultures and national origins. While the parents may have been eager to maintain the home language, surely in part to be able to maintain discipline and the flow of communication within the home, their children had another agenda. Among the children of immigrants, English emerged as an unequivocal winner in the struggle for their linguistic souls. As we noted in Chapter 2, this is also true among today's immigrant youth. In the facetious words of Harvard sociologist Stanley Lieberson and his colleagues, the United States is "a cemetery" for languages.[21]

Third- and fourth-generation descendants of earlier waves of European immigrants have made an effort in recent years to regain lost linguistic traditions. In Massachusetts, fourth-generation monolingual English-speaking parents are sending their youngsters to special after-school classes and tutors to learn such languages as Yiddish and Lithuanian. These attempts at resuscitation reveal the powerful emotional appeal of language as a symbol of identity.

What should we know about bilingualism in children to generate rational and coherent policy? In reality, very few people can be considered "balanced" bilinguals. Most bilingual speakers are in fact dominant in one language. For other bilinguals, language use is divided according to specific domains: family and emotional matters may be most comfortably expressed in one language, while conversations about work may be most fluently discussed in another. Still other bilinguals engage in a linguistic flow characterized by strategically switching between the two languages depending upon the context and need.[22]

Bilingual skills fall along a continuum; most so-called bilinguals might be more properly called emerging bilinguals. In reality, balanced bilingualism is quite an achievement.[23] It requires a lot of effort to learn a second language well. Once mastery is achieved, regular use is necessary to maintain it. At the same time, much effort is required to keep up the original language through frequent use. Language skills atrophy quickly if not exercised on a regular basis. A real danger to cognitive development occurs when children rapidly lose their first language without receiving adequate training and practice in the new language.

How do immigrant students acquire a second language? Research in second-language acquisition suggests that the best predictor of success is the skill amassed in the child's first language. It seems that cognitive skills developed in the first language can greatly assist in the learning of the second. Hence, a Spanish-speaking child who has a good mastery of the vocabulary and metalinguistic aspects of her first language will find her transition into English much easier than someone with underdeveloped linguistic skills in her first language.[24]

A common myth is that young children learn a second language effortlessly and better than older speakers. This is simply not true. In fact, all things being equal, an older speaker will tend to learn a second language faster than a younger speaker does.[25] Young children will, however, do better than older learners in speaking the new language without an easily detectable foreign accent.

While there are individual differences among school-age children, full academic mastery of a second language usually takes between six and seven years of study and exposure.[26] Linguistically gifted children who are systematically exposed to good language models may achieve mastery in two to three years. It is important to note the profound difference between having a superficial conversational ability in a language and having the deeper level of competence required to understand difficult new subjects, to express subtleties of meaning, and to write a well-argued and well-phrased term paper.

Another common myth concerning bilingualism is that native language use at home interferes with the acquisition of a second language at school. In a state-of-the-art review of bilingualism and second-language learning sponsored by the National Research Council, language scholars Diane August and Kenji Hakuta conclude: "The use of the child's native language does not impede the acquisition of English."[27]

In fact, children who speak two languages may have special advantages. Some scholars emphasize the obvious job-market advantage of speaking more than one language.[28] Others see bilingual speakers as having an edge in the cognitive and interpersonal realms. Bilinguals may develop greater skill and empathy in dealing with people from a variety of backgrounds. Some have argued that by shifting from one code to another, bilinguals may also develop cognitive flexibilities that allow them to approach other new language tasks more creatively.[29] Still other scholars point to the aesthetic value of being able to easily navigate linguistic boundaries.[30] In general, research suggests that bilinguals may have special advantages in "their overall linguistic, cognitive, or social development" over monolinguals of the same socioeconomic background.[31]

Bilingual education has been controversial ever since it was created. In 1968 President Lyndon Johnson signed the Bilingual Education Act to provide educational support to poor children who were "educationally disadvantaged because of their inability to speak English."[32] It did not mandate first-language instruction and allowed for a wide range of interpretations and implementations. A few years later, the historic Supreme Court ruling on *Lau v. Nichols* mandated special school assistance to San Francisco's largest immigrant groups—Chinese, Filipinos, and Latinos—without spelling out how the assistance was to be implemented. The debate over whether the goal of bilingual education is to provide transitional support or to produce individuals who are bilingual and biliterate is far from settled.

Under the rubric of bilingual education, we find a wide variety of programs and practices.[33] In some school settings, "bilingual education" is nothing more than teaching children in English and minimally modifying the curriculum by simplifying vocabulary so that they can understand the lesson. Such programs are sometimes termed "structured immersion." Other schools offer "sheltered English" programs, where "every lesson in every school subject becomes, in part, a language lesson."[34] With "sheltered English," a science lesson is also an English lesson. English as a Second Language programs typically consist of a daily pull-out period where the child is taught the basics of English; the rest of her day may be spent in an immersion setting.[35]

In other schools, we find so-called transitional bilingual education programs. In these settings the child is provided with structured English-language instruction. At the same time, the child is taught a variety of subjects in her native language until she achieves competence in English. At that time she will be moved to an English-only classroom. The idea behind this model is to keep the child from falling behind in other subjects while she is mastering English.[36] Yet other programs come under the rubric of "two-way bilingual education."[37] In such programs, children are taught in their native language alongside English monolingual students who are motivated to learn a foreign language. In theory, all students receive the same amount of instruction in both languages in a variety of subject matters.

Scholars of second-language acquisition argue that two-way bilingual programs tend to be effective for a variety of reasons. In such settings, language-minority children are in intimate, systematic, and reciprocal contact with speakers of the dominant language who provide good language models—a critical ingredient for effective second-language acquisition.[38] Furthermore, being surrounded by native-born dominant-language speakers who value learning a second language can act as a partial antidote to negative social mirroring.

Bilingual education has had strong critics since its initial legislation. While some object to the costs involved in such programs, others are philosophically opposed to the idea of teaching language-minority children in American schools using a language other than English. These critics fear that teaching children in a language other than English will undermine the American culture and doom students to academic failure, eventually handicapping them in the job market.

But does bilingual education really threaten American mainstream culture? We have already reviewed the research that shows how most immigrant children shift quickly into using English and lose their first language. Furthermore, the idea that immigrant languages pose a threat to English, and hence to the unity of the country, ignores the fact that English is a pervasive and highly influential language both at home and on the world stage. Never before has a language reached the dominance that English has achieved in the realms of business and commerce, science and technology, and media and popular culture.[39]

The issue of whether or not children in bilingual programs are handicapped in their academic progress is more complex. Research considering the efficacy of bilingual programs reveals contradictory results. This should not be surprising given that there are nearly as many models of bilingual and language assistance programs as there are districts in the country. It is therefore natural to find that while some programs produce excellent results, others are plagued with problems.[40]

The research suggests that while some bilingual programs are successful, others are characterized by poor administrative support, inadequate resources, and uncertified personnel. Under the best of circumstances it is a challenge to educate large numbers of immigrant students. Indeed many of the problems found in bilingual programs tend to mask other issues. Many of the children in such programs come from poor backgrounds, have had little or interrupted schooling in their country of origin, move often from district to district, and are dealing with the trauma or losses involved in the immigrant journey. These children would face academic difficulties whether or not they were enrolled in a bilingual program. Blaming their slow progress on the bilingual program they attend ignores the many other difficulties that these children face. The paradox of bilingual education is that it is asked to do more with less. Bilingual programs must educate children, many of whom have a variety of special needs. It is an investment in the future—one that is in most cases supported half-heartedly—for which there is little immediate apparent payback.

Many bilingual programs have real problems in their implementation. Perhaps the most common problem in the day-to-day running of bilingual programs is the dearth of fully certified bilingual teachers who are trained in second-language acquisition and who can serve as proper language models to their students. It is a challenge to find qualified teachers even for such popular languages as Mandarin, Cantonese, and Spanish. In California, emergency credentialing is routine. Some districts in desperate need of qualified teachers have recruited in Spain and South America. While these teachers speak Spanish, in some cases their English skills (grammar, vocabulary, and accent) are inadequate. Furthermore, most of these teachers are neither familiar with teaching in an American setting nor aware of the cultural and historical backgrounds of the immigrant students. In districts where children arrive speaking a hundred different languages, it is virtually impossible to find qualified bilingual teachers.

In the course of our research, we have found that children whose native language is Fujianese must first master Cantonese on their way to learning English because their bilingual classrooms are taught in a Cantonese and English. In other classrooms, we saw how immigrant youngsters who had been here a bit longer come to function as de facto teacher's aides. While this has clear advantages for the teacher and may help such children develop confidence, there are costs. It has been reported that in some bilingual programs, children have been kept from advancing into mainstream classes because teachers need them to help newly arrived immigrant students.[41] Furthermore, because the somewhat more advanced students typically have limited English skills themselves, newly arrived students are not receiving ideal language modeling.

There is a danger in segregating large numbers of immigrant students into bilingual programs.[42] First, in most such programs, children have almost no meaningful contact with English-speaking peers; without such contact, an important source of linguistic modeling is wasted. Moreover, because many bilingual programs are ambivalently supported throughout the nation, they simply do not offer the breadth and depth of courses that immigrant students need to prepare for college. Bilingual high school science courses with very basic content and limited lab access, for example, may not provide the necessary foundations to succeed once the student has acquired sufficient English to enroll in a more advanced class. Hence, there is an ever-present danger that once a student enters the "ESL" or "bilingual" track, she will have difficulty switching to the college-bound track.

The irrefutable reality is that large-scale immigration generates special needs that cannot be addressed with easy shortcuts. Immigrant children require special help with English.[43] Learning a second language takes time and effort. Yet while children are mastering English, they must keep up with the content of their classes so that by the time they can function in English they are not hopelessly behind in their other subjects. Bilingual education at its best can assure that children prosper academically and develop and maintain competencies in two linguistic realms.

SCHOOL REFORM

In 1997 California voters, dissatisfied with bilingual education, passed Proposition 227—thereby dismantling overnight bilingual programs in the state with the largest enrollment of immigrant students in the nation. The discontent with bilingual education is part of a broader, more general concern about the quality of our schools and their ability to prepare our children for the global economy.[44]

These concerns have led to a variety of efforts that have come to be known generally as "school reform." They include such varied policy initiatives as increased graduation requirements, systematic assessments through "objective tests," "school choice," and "inclusion." Some researchers have pointed out that such efforts, while often undertaken to improve the quality of education for all children, may ultimately benefit middle-class students but do little, and may even harm, the academic progress of children who come from poorer homes, whose parents have little education, and who are English-language learners.[45]

The rush to do away with bilingual education in California exemplifies the serious problems, as well as the negative possible consequences, of these new policy initiatives. Under Proposition 227 teachers were mandated to "immerse" second-language learners in an "English only" environment. The idea is that an intense one-year immersion program is enough to bring second-language learners to the point where they can fully function academically in English. But as we already noted, the scientific literature on second-language acquisition clearly shows that this takes more than a year to achieve. To make matters worse, teachers in California received very limited preparation, training, or appropriate materials (including textbooks) to teach their non-English-speaking students. In essence the old programs, both good and bad, were eradicated without first providing an appropriate replacement.

Likewise, what is perhaps the centerpiece in the new wave of educational reform—increasing high school graduation requirements and introducing high-stakes testing as a graduation requirement—will have a far-reaching effect on large numbers of immigrant students. A number of studies suggest that immigrant high school students who do not have adequate English to enroll in mainstream classes end up in classes that neither count toward the new graduation requirements nor prepare them for the tests needed to graduate. Under such circumstances, many immigrant high school students will drop out.[46]

High-stakes testing is another popular wave in the current school reform movement. The frequent use of standardized tests generates special problems for immigrant students. Yet performance on these tests will significantly influence the student's future. Some states are requiring that all students pass an examination before being allowed to graduate from high school. In addition, in what has become a dreaded yearly ritual, school districts compare the performance of their students to that of students in other districts based solely on the use of standardized tests. In many districts pressure to do well on these assessments is reshaping teaching practice and curriculum, with valuable class time devoted to "teach to the test."

Such testing has come under heavy criticism—a complex issue that is beyond the scope of this book. It is relevant here, however, to point out the problems that these assessment tools pose for immigrant students. These measures are typically developed and normed on "mainstream" students. Many of these tests are not only *not* "culture free" but are indeed "culture bound." Tests pose questions that are often framed around issues and content not as familiar to immigrant children as to children brought up in the dominant culture. Language difficulties compound the problem of a timed test for some immigrant students because such children simply take longer to read materials intended for English monolinguals.[47]

Two other school reform initiatives bear mention. "School choice" is designed to allow parents to enroll their children in schools of their choice. To date there is no evidence to suggest that large numbers of the very best schools would be eager to develop curriculum to serve significant numbers of poor immigrant students. Furthermore, recently arrived immigrant parents are often not knowledgeable about placing their children in these "choice" schools, nor do they have the resources to do so. While well-networked middle-class parents are poised to take advantage of these choices, many poor immigrant parents are left with no choice at all.[48]

"Inclusion" is used to describe incorporating children with special needs in regular classrooms. Children with physical disabilities (such as those who are visually impaired or confined to wheelchairs) or with learning disorders (such as children diagnosed with dyslexia or Asperger's Syndrome) fall into this category. Little data exist on how "inclusion" works for language minority students with physical or learning disabilities. Certainly, inclusion requires ongoing efforts to integrate and support these students as they strive to become a dynamic part of the class. Teachers working with such students often need specialized training and support to provide adequate service to their students. The progress of the students must be regularly assessed to determine that they are indeed receiving the support they need.[49]

We need to be cautious when carrying out school reform efforts. From our perspective, a basic weakness in all of these efforts is that they do not fully recognize the experiences and needs of *immigrant* children. The models for these school reform efforts have as a common denominator the experiences of middle-class mainstream children. This is not an insignificant oversight given that immigrant youth are the fastest growing sector of our student population.

These policies have the potential to shape academic opportunities for immigrant students. Yet through ethnography we have learned that abstract educational policies are often not implemented in classrooms in ways that help immigrant students. And what takes place in the classroom has an immediate effect on the child's experiences, behaviors, and developing attitudes.

Classroom Engagement

When an immigrant child finally sits at her desk in her new classroom, a world of possibilities can open. In some classrooms, immigrant children will flourish. During the course of our fieldwork, we have observed classrooms where teachers constructively engage their students' energies, optimism, and willingness to work hard. Children in these classrooms are surrounded by peers who recognize and support the crucial role of school in their future well-being. They are exposed to a curriculum that presents meaningful ideas in creative ways, and they have access to instructional technologies and other up-to-date classroom materials.

In other cases, we have found classrooms where teachers are resentful and feel burdened by their new charges, convey pessimism about the immigrant students' abilities to learn, and fail to engage them. In such classrooms, immigrant children come in contact with many peers who have given up on school and are regularly disruptive. "Classroom management techniques"—a euphemism for discipline—consume teachers' energies. Textbooks are either out-of-date or way above students' reading skills, and much of the class time is spent filling out dull and meaningless worksheets. In these classrooms students often are not engaged with their teachers or with the materials they are supposed to master. Over time, the outcomes are predictable. In the poignant words of Stanford researcher Guadalupe Valdéz, "During the course of the year, the eagerness of the newly arrived youngsters gave way to vacant expressions. The students who had looked forward eagerly to school in the United States were disappointed. Even *they* knew that they were not making much progress."[50]

Perhaps the most important challenge that takes place within the classroom is facilitating the child's ability to build on the cognitive skills that she brings with her to the new setting. Because most immigrant children arrive at the classroom with very limited English skills, cognitive competencies may be masked. While the student may be able to work at fairly advanced levels in her native language, her inability to speak English will make it difficult for her to cover the same materials in the new language. Many immigrant children in our study report feeling frustrated that they are now going over materials they had mastered in their native language long ago. A Central American high school student noted that while he was learning English, his teachers always asked "the same question— things you already know. So you don't learn new stuff." A middle-school Mexican boy expressed his frustration: "I am learning again what I already knew in Mexico and I get bored in class."

Some parents also express concerns that their children have not been challenged in their new schools. A Chinese mother complained that her son was not being encouraged to learn new material, despite moving to one of the highest-ranked schools in the Boston area. "School is mainly a place for kids to interact with other kids. [My son] does not really learn much from his teachers." A Dominican father noted, "I think classes should be more challenging. Homework should be expected *and* corrected. Teachers should pay more attention to student's achievements. I would think that there are greater expectations for white American [students]."

As immigrant children progress in their acquisition of English skills, learning can accelerate. Over time, much will depend on whether the teacher can engage children who are often linguistically as well as culturally different from herself. A number of studies suggest that teachers who are able to teach in culturally relevant ways are better equipped to engage immigrant children and produce better results in learning, student morale, and classroom dynamics.[51]

In exploring the issue of culture in the classroom, three significant matters should be kept in mind. First is the issue of culturally and linguistically meaningful materials. If a child cannot understand, she will not be able to identify with and emotionally invest in a given topic; in such circumstances, meaningful learning cannot occur. Efforts to make curricular materials relevant to the social and cultural experiences of children engage interest and generate enthusiasm.

In a Boston area school, an extraordinarily gifted teacher introduced his newly arrived immigrant students to statistical concepts by developing a special project about immigration. They drew on their own immigrant experiences, which were then used to examine broad patterns in the history of immigration to the United States. Soon, young students were charting the mean number of immigrants arriving in the United States every year, the top countries of origin, and the main cities where immigrants tend to settle. Teachers who introduce cultural materials that provide a familiar mirror to their students will be rewarded by their enthusiasm and joy in learning.

A related theme is the issue of the discontinuities that immigrant children experience as they move from classrooms in their countries of origin to American classrooms. Beyond the obvious linguistic and curricular differences, children must learn to navigate in classrooms that are dominated by different cultural styles. Many immigrant children are used to classrooms that are highly structured and require cognitive and interpersonal practices that are quite different from what is expected in the typical American classroom. When visiting classrooms in countries where our informants come from, we witnessed children seated in symmetrically arranged rows facing the teacher, who stood at the front of the classroom, chalk in hand, making the children repeat in unison memorized materials. In such classrooms the authority of the teacher is unchallenged; in some cases corporal punishment is an ever-present threat.

When we asked children what they found different about American schools, many were quick to comment on the distinct classroom practices. A fifteen-year-old Chinese girl noted: "Here [in the United States] I am more open. I have the courage to raise my hand if I know something. If something funny happens I will laugh. I will talk in class. I did not dare do these things when I was in Canton." A nine-year-old Dominican boy told us: "There everybody was afraid of the teachers, but here we are not." A twelve-year-old Haitian boy wryly advised us: "In Haiti, they beat the kids in school . . . [Here] it is the teachers who get beat up, not the kids."

Classrooms in the United States are dominated, however superficially, by an ethos of egalitarianism and democracy. The immigrant child may initially come to experience the new social pace and structure as disorienting. In some classrooms, students are expected to address their teachers by their first names, a practice that many immigrant children and parents find incomprehensible. Cultural miscommunication easily ensues. Guadalupe Valdéz, in a study of immigrant children in a California school, found that immigrant children "who were used to teachers who are strict and who demand both silence and respect, had trouble reading the signals of those teachers who seem nice, who wanted to be liked, and who wanted to make learning fun."[52]

School and Parent Relations

Just as the potential for miscommunication is ever present between teachers and students in the classroom, the relationships among teachers, staff, and parents are likewise quite complex and often reveal tensions and misunderstandings. While in general newly arrived immigrant parents tend to be positive about the schooling opportunities afforded to their children, there is one area where they hold deep reservations about the American system. Many, if not most, come to abhor the lack of discipline and respect they see in their children's new schools. American children are viewed as disrespectful of elders, and authority figures and teachers are considered weak and ineffectual in maintaining discipline and order.

There are other areas of conflict and misunderstanding based on differences in cultural expectations. In many cultural settings, there is a somewhat rigid social boundary separating the realm of school from the realm of home. In the United States, there is more fluidity and parents are expected to be active partners in their children's schooling. Teachers and administrators expect parents to participate in a host of social activities such as in Parent Teacher Associations, as volunteers in classrooms, and as fund-raisers. Parents are expected to be involved in school projects and homework assignments and to advocate for their children. When asked what she saw as her biggest challenge in dealing with immigrant parents, a charismatic principal replied, "They need to become *advocates* in their children's schooling."

Immigrant parents arrive with very different cultural models and expectations than those found among mainstream American parents. There are important cultural differences between groups; indeed the expectations of Haitian parents are quite different from those of Chinese parents. Nevertheless, there is a common denominator in the general attitudes and expectations among a broad range of immigrant parents. First, many immigrant parents believe that it is not their business to micromanage the schooling of their children. We have found a general belief among many immigrant parents that teachers are responsible for what goes on in school. This is true among both high-status and low-status immigrant parents. Many parents note that it would be presumptuous for them to second-guess teachers' decisions and behaviors. Second, these beliefs tend to be compounded by the fact that immigrants, as social outsiders, feel less secure about questioning the judgment of school authorities. This is especially true for parents who have themselves had little formal schooling and are thus less savvy about the culture of "going to school."

Beyond these cultural differences, immediate social factors constrain how present many immigrant parents can be in their children's schools. For parents working two or three jobs, it is simply impossible to attend school activities in the middle of the day as teachers often expect. Lack of English skills among many immigrant parents makes the expected participation in school activities quite problematic. Lower-status immigrant parents with little formal schooling may feel self-conscious and socially uncomfortable when interacting with authority figures in schools. Undocumented parents must overcome other barriers; the ever-present fear of being caught by the INS is sometimes generalized to all authorities, including school personnel.

Many teachers interpret the general "hands-off" approach to schooling among many immigrant parents as lack of interest in the child's school progress. Nothing could be further from the truth. As we have already suggested, for the vast majority of immigrant parents the opportunities afforded by schooling in the new country are a highly valued gift.

In fact, for many immigrant parents, their admiration and trust of the schools turn out to be double-edged. Some immigrant parents, especially those escaping very poor and violence-ridden countries, come to believe that their children are succeeding in school simply because they are able to attend school daily without the interruptions brought about by warfare or lack of funding. For others, the fact that school is free and children are given books and sometimes breakfast and lunch is proof positive that they live in a bountiful country where opportunities will be provided for their children.

Parental Savvy about School Differences

While early on immigrant parents tend to become intoxicated with the prospects that schooling seems to provide their children, over time they may develop a more sober understanding. Their initial anxieties and ambivalence about discipline become more generalized. Parents who begin to focus more attentively on what is happening in schools worry that their children are going over materials they had learned years ago. Over time, as knowledge circulates through immigrant networks, parents are better able to understand the finer distinctions between types of schools as well as types of educational programs within schools and the different paths they lead to. At this point, immigrant parents who can afford to will move to better districts and will enroll their children in schools that promise them a better program of study. Others begin to worry about making sure that their children are taking the right courses that will get them into a good college.

Herein lies the critical role that parents can and indeed must learn to play in the education of their children. Many immigrant parents will discover that it is dangerous to put too much trust in an educational system that produces such uneven results. The very best and the very worst that American schooling has to offer can be found within a thirty-mile radius of most major cities. Learning this information requires an active effort for newcomers.

In order to gain access to better educational opportunities for their children, parents must learn the new rules of engagement in a very complex, high-stakes game. They need to know things that middle-class college-educated parents take for granted: the difference between college-track and non-college-track courses, preparing for the PSAT and SAT, differences in opportunities afforded by attending different colleges (junior colleges, four-year colleges, and universities), how to write a college application essay, and how to access financial aid.

In short, immigrant students and their parents must learn about the educational requirements for various careers as well as how to access that education in the new land. Guidance counselors should play a major role in this regard, but as it stands today, they often do not. Caseloads for guidance counselors are staggeringly large, and funding is inadequate. Further, many guidance counselors are out of touch with the realities of the new economy. They frequently misinterpret linguistic difficulties as indicating a lack of intelligence or "college potential" and track immigrant students into non-college course sequences. Even high-achieving immigrant students are sometimes locked out of the better colleges either by being overlooked or through active subversion by their guidance counselors. We have been told by Ivy League affirmative action recruiters that some guidance counselors even act as gatekeepers by writing negative evaluations of even their gifted and hard-working immigrant students.

Mastering the rules of the new game is an essential ingredient of parental empowerment, but in some cases it is not enough. The structural barriers of poor, crowded, and violent schools with no meaningful curriculum or pedagogy are for many, especially low-status immigrants, simply too much to overcome. Massive investment in troubled schools is needed to update materials, properly train and supervise certified teachers, shrink classroom size, and make teachers and administrators more accountable to the students—and families—they serve. Providing culturally sensitive information to immigrant families about how they can ensure that their children will receive a solid education clearly should be a policy goal.

While many immigrant children face serious obstacles in their schooling, their optimism, positive attitudes, and willingness to work hard in many cases act as a powerful counterforce even in less than optimal schools. Immigrant families, as a rule, strongly believe in the importance of schooling. And research suggests that parents can make a tremendous difference.[53]

A charismatic mentor can also play a decisive role. We have seen how a caring baseball coach who explicitly instructs his Dominican protégés in the "rules of the game" (both in the field and in life) made an immense difference in the careers of his immigrant students.

Finally, let us never underestimate the powerful influence a teacher can have in a child's life. Albert Camus, himself an immigrant, grew up in a poor neighborhood in Algiers, without a father and with a deaf and mute mother. He went on to write one of the most widely celebrated novels of the twentieth century. A few months after receiving the Nobel Prize for literature in 1957, he wrote to his teacher Monsieur Germain:

> I let the commotion around me these days subside a bit before speaking to you from the bottom of my heart. I have just been given far too great an honor, one I neither sought nor solicited. But when I heard the news, my first thought, after my mother, was of you. Without you, without the affectionate hand you extended to the small poor child that I was, without your teaching, and your example, none of this would have happened. I don't make too much of this sort of honor. But at least it gives me an opportunity to tell you what you have been and still are for me, and to assure you that your efforts, your work, and the generous heart you put into it still live in one of your little schoolboys who, despite the years, has never stopped being your grateful pupil. I embrace you with all my heart.[54]

As we face the largest wave of immigration in the history of the United States, much attention has been focused on its economic and policy implications.[1] This focus, while important, can be limiting. In the final analysis, if that is ever possible in this field, the economic implications of large-scale immigration turn out to be marginal. The U.S. economy is so large, powerful, and dynamic that most responsible economists do not think immigration will either "make or break" it. The recent public concern about immigration seems, therefore, out of proportion to its importance for our economy. We must conclude that the intensity of public concern reveals more deep-seated, personal anxieties.

We suspect that these anxieties have to do with the demographic and cultural implications of a wave of immigration made up largely of non-European, non-English-speaking people of color migrating in large numbers from Asia, the Caribbean, and Latin America. Many concerns are being raised—some vehemently and others quite reasonably. What will this wave of immigration do to the culture of our nation? What will the ethos of the country "feel like" by the mid-twenty-first century, when the children of today's immigrants and other racial minorities constitute nearly half of its population? And the bottom line: Will the country suffer or be better off because of this historic shift?

While important policy questions need to be addressed, such as how many immigrants the United States should accept each year, what kinds of publicly funded services they can access, and how to

stem continuing waves of undocumented immigration, in some respects much of this debate is academic. The proverbial horse is out
of the barn and closing the door now, even if it would be symbolically satisfying to some, will in practice have little effect.

Immigration, especially from Latin America and the Caribbean,
will continue. The experience of the last three decades has taught us
that immigration is structured by extremely powerful and global social, economic, and cultural factors that democratic nations cannot
easily regulate with unilateral policy initiatives. The anemic results
of policies such as the multibillion-dollar border control efforts now
in place, California's Proposition 187, and the array of recent federal
legislation affecting the services that immigrants can access reveal
just how difficult it is to contain immigration.

The more relevant question at the beginning of the new millennium is how we can best incorporate into our society the large number of immigrants who now call the United States their home.[2] Nowhere is the need to responsibly address these issues greater than
when it comes to immigrant children. How can we ease their transition and adaptation to the American setting? How can we harness
their energies and prepare them for the future? How do we make
sure that they grow up to be citizens who contribute to the public
good? Schooling is at the heart of all these questions.[3]

The current wave of immigration coincided with the "tax revolt"
that led to massive cutbacks in education.[4] These cutbacks resulted
in overcrowded classrooms, unmanageable counselor-student ratios,
and outdated materials. Not surprisingly, poor schools in poor districts were most negatively affected by these initiatives. These were
precisely the schools where poor immigrant children enrolled in
large numbers.

Three decades after the tax revolt, there is now a consensus that
our educational system is in crisis. Since the late 1990s, education
has emerged as the number one public concern—ahead of the economy and crime. While different observers of the educational system have proposed an array of possible solutions, there is a general
agreement that reinvesting in the schooling of children is a crucial
first step. It is important to recognize that immigrant children are a

growing sector of the school population; policy interventions and funding decisions must be attuned to their special needs. If immigrant children are well served today, they will become important contributors to the future well-being of our country.

To date, the attention focused on immigrant children and their families has been largely misplaced. To paraphrase the Israeli statesman Abba Eban, "Those who oppose immigration never miss an opportunity to miss an opportunity."

Consider, for example, the ever-present concern that immigrant children are not learning English and therefore not acculturating to the United States. There are two fundamental problems with this commonly held belief. First, it runs counter to the now nearly overwhelming evidence that immigrant children are learning English as quickly and well as they always have—if not faster. At the same time, unfortunately, immigrant children are rapidly losing their native languages.[5] Second, the link between learning English and "acculturation" rests on a superficial and reductionistic assumption that speaking English equals acculturation. But simply speaking English does not make one an American.[6] To reduce culture to the acquisition of a second language misses the great depth of what culture is in terms of values, worldviews, and social practices.

Some of our concerns about acculturation rest on a deep flaw in the understanding of culture. Analytically, we differentiate between two broad realms of culture: "instrumental culture" and "expressive culture." By instrumental culture, we mean the skills, competencies, and social behaviors that are required to successfully make a living and contribute to society. By expressive culture, we mean the realm of values, worldviews, and patterning of interpersonal relations that give meaning and sustain the sense of self. Taken together, these qualities of culture generate shared meanings, shared understandings, and a sense of belonging. In sum, the sense of who you are and where you belong is molded by these qualities of culture.

In the instrumental realm, there is arguably a worldwide convergence in the skills that are needed to function in today's global economy. Whether they live in Los Angeles, Lima, or Lagos, workers need communication, symbolic, and technical skills as well as good work habits and interpersonal talent.

Immigrant parents are very aware that if their children are to thrive they must acquire these skills. Indeed, immigration for many parents represents nothing more, and nothing less, than the opportunity to offer children access to these skills. We have yet to meet an immigrant parent who says that he does not want his child to learn English or to acquire the skills and work habits that will prepare him or her for a successful career in the United States or "back home."

While immigrant parents encourage their children to cultivate the "instrumental" aspects of culture in the new setting, they are decidedly more ambivalent about their children's exposure to some of the "expressive" elements in the new land. During the course of our research, it has been obvious to us that many immigrant parents strongly resist a whole array of cultural models and social practices in American youth culture that they consider highly undesirable. These include cultural attitudes and behaviors that are anti-schooling ("school is boring") and anti-authority ("the principal is an idiot"), the glorification of violence, and sexually precocious behaviors. Immigrant parents, rightly, reject and resist this form of acculturation.

We claim that the incantation of many observers—acculturate, acculturate, acculturate—needs rethinking. If acculturation is superficially defined as acquiring linguistic skills and job skills, then there is a universal consensus on these shared goals. If, on the other hand, we choose a broader, more realistic, definition of acculturation that includes the realm of values, worldviews, and interpersonal relations, then a worthy debate ensues.

The first issue that needs airing is the basic question of "acculturating to what?" American society is no longer, if it ever was, a uniform or coherent system.[7] Given their diverse origins, financial resources, and social networks, immigrants gravitate to very different sectors of American society. While some are able to join integrated well-to-do neighborhoods, the majority of today's immigrants come to experience American culture from the vantage point of poor urban neighborhoods. Limited economic opportunities, ethnic tensions, violence, drugs, and gangs characterize many of these settings. The structural inequalities found in what some social theorists have called "American Apartheid" are implicated in the creation of a cultural ethos of ambivalence, pessimism, and despair.[8] Asking immigrant youth to give up their values, worldviews, and interpersonal relations to join this ethos is a formula for disaster.

For those immigrants who come into intimate contact with middle-class mainstream culture, other trade-offs will be required. As our data suggest, immigrant children perceive that mainstream Americans do not welcome them and, indeed, disparage them as not deserving to partake in the American dream. Identifying wholeheartedly with a culture that rejects you has its psychological costs, usually paid with the currency of shame, doubt, and even self-hatred.

But even if the new immigrants were unambivalently embraced by middle-class mainstream Americans, it is far from clear that mimicking mainstream behaviors would in the long term prove to be an adaptive strategy for immigrants of color. Mainstream middle-class children are protected by social safety nets that give them leeway to experiment with an array of dysfunctional behaviors including drugs, early sexual relations, and alcohol. But for the many immigrant youth who do not have robust socioeconomic and cultural safety nets, engaging in such behaviors is a high-stakes proposition where one mistake can have life-long consequences. While a white middle-class youth that is caught in possession of drugs is likely to be referred to counseling and rehabilitation, an immigrant youth convicted of the same offense may be deported.

The current wave of immigration involves people from diverse and heterogeneous cultural backgrounds. Yet beneath surface differences, a common grammar can be identified among groups as culturally distinct from each other as Chinese, Haitian, and Mexican immigrants. The importance of family ties, an emphasis on hard work, and optimism about the future are examples of shared immigrant values that are deepened during immigration.[9] Consider, for example, the case of strong family ties among immigrants. Many immigrants come from cultures where the family system is an integral part of the person's sense of self. These family ties play a critical role in family reunification—an important force driving the new immigration. Furthermore, once immigrants settle, family ties are accentuated because immigration's emotional and practical challenges force family members to turn to one another for support. Immigrant families do not need to be lectured by opportunistic politicians about family values—they embody them.

Hard work and optimism about the future are likewise central to the immigrant's raison d'être. The immigrant's most fundamental motivation is to find a better life. Immigrants tend to view hard work as essential to this project. That some immigrants will do the impossible jobs that native workers simply refuse to consider indicates just how hard they are willing to work. The strong family ties and work ethic of immigrants, as well as their optimism about the future, are unique assets that should be celebrated as adding to the total cultural stock of the nation.

Immigration generates change. As we have argued in this book, the immigrants themselves undergo a variety of transformations. Likewise, immigration inevitably changes the members of the dominant culture. In the United States today we eat, speak, and dance differently than we did thirty years ago, in part because of large-scale immigration. But change is never easy. The changes brought about by the new immigration require mutual accommodation and negotiation.

Rather than advocating that immigrant children abandon all elements of their culture as they embark on their uncertain journey, a more promising path is to cultivate and nurture the emergence of new hybrid identities and bicultural competencies.[10] These hybrid cultural styles creatively blend elements of the old culture with that of the new, unleashing new energies and potentials.[11]

The skills and work habits that are required to thrive in the new century are essential elements of acculturation. Immigrant children, like all children, must develop this repertoire of instrumental skills.

At the same time, maintaining a sense of belonging and social cohesion with their immigrant roots is equally important. When immigrant children lose their expressive culture, social cohesion is weakened, parental authority is undermined, and interpersonal relations suffer. The unthinking call for immigrant children to massively abandon their culture can only result in loss, anomie, and social disruption.

The model of unilineal acculturation–where the bargain was straightforward: please check all your cultural baggage before you pass through the Golden Gate—emerged in another era.[12] The young nation was then eager to turn large numbers of European immigrants into loyal citizen workers and consumers. It was an era of nation-building and of bounded national projects.

But even then, despite what we may have learned in history books, immigrants did not rush in unison to trade their culture for American culture. German Americans, Italian Americans, and Irish Americans have all left deep cultural imprints in American culture. Even among fifth-generation descendants of the previous great wave of immigration, symbolic culture and ethnicity remain an emotional center.[13]

But beyond the argument that maintaining the expressive elements of culture supports social cohesion, there is another argument worth considering. In the global era, the tenets of unilineal acculturation are no longer relevant. Today there are clear and unequivocal advantages to being able to operate in multiple cultural codes—as anyone working in a major (and now not-so-major) corporation knows. There are social, economic, cognitive and aesthetic advantages to being able to transverse cultural spaces. Immigrant children are poised to maximize that unique advantage. While many view these children's cultural–including linguistic—skills as a threat, we see them as precious assets to be cultivated.

A renowned historian once said that the history of the United States is fundamentally the history of immigration.[14] Throughout history, U.S. citizens have ambivalently welcomed newcomers. The fear then, as now, focused on whether the immigrants would contribute to the American project. The gift of hindsight demonstrates just how essential immigration has been to the making and remaking of America. Welcoming and supporting new generations of immigrants to the United States will ensure that this vital legacy continues.

INTRODUCTION

1. See Kao and Tienda 1995; Hernandez and Charney 1998; Rumbaut 1995, pp. 46–48; S. Steinberg 1996; and C. Suárez-Orozco and M. Suárez-Orozco 1995.

2. See, for example, Orfield and Yun 1999.

3. Landale and Oropesa 1995.

4. Portes 1993.

5. Maira 1998.

6. Portes 1993.

7. Yet other immigrant groups seem to approximate the norms of the majority population—"disappearing" into American institutions and culture without much notice.

8. See Kao and Tienda 1995; Rumbaut 1995; Steinberg, Brown, and Dornbusch 1996; C. Suárez-Orozco and M. Suárez-Orozco 1995.

9. Hernandez and Charney 1998, quote from p. 159.

10. Rumbaut 1996.

11. Rumbaut 1995.

12. Quoted in Suro 1998, p. 13.

13. Quoted in Olsen 1998, p. 68.

14. This is a study in progress. In this book, we will be drawing on the first year of data from the project. While it is tempting to digress about the methodological challenges in the conception, development, and execution of a project of this magnitude, doing so is beyond the scope of this book. Future publications will elaborate on those aspects of the Harvard Immigration Project.

15. Large numbers of immigrant children are undocumented, a legal status that, as we examine later, has important implications for their daily experiences and opportunities in the new society.

16. Participating children were required to have been born abroad, and

to have spent at least two-thirds of their life in the country of origin prior to migration. At the beginning of the study, the children ranged in ages from 9 to 14 with a mean age of 11.77. The sample is balanced by gender.

17. While we have claimed that it is important to differentiate analytically between foreign-born and U.S.-born children, it is also clear that there are important commonalities between the two, which we explore especially in Chapter 4 when we discuss identity issues.

18. Acculturation theory predicted that as immigrants gravitated toward American culture they would acquire "the memories, sentiments, and attitudes" of members of the dominant culture (see Park and Burgess 1969, p. 735). Milton Gordon (1964) saw immigrant acculturation as a unilinear journey toward the acquisition of "middle class cultural patterns of, largely, white Protestant, Anglo-Saxon origins" (72). At the heart of this theory is the idea that over time immigrants had to shed much of their cultural baggage—including language, values and worldviews. This was seen as a positive development: immigrants, especially their children, were thought to better themselves immensely through Americanization. Whatever immigrants lost was clearly outweighed by the great gains they achieved. Today social theorists seem to be more interested in examining the processes of change brought about by immigration as a dynamic of transculturation where all groups involved–including the majority group—make mutual cultural adjustments and calibrations. For various theoretical statements on the topic of acculturation see, inter alia, Park 1930; Gordon 1964; and Alba and Nee 1997.

ONE   THE VARIETIES OF IMMIGRANT EXPERIENCE

1. To protect the confidentiality of our informants, all names are pseudonyms.

2. More recently we have witnessed the emergence of gender-based variables as an important factor for seeking asylum in a safe country. Radical female mutilation has emerged as possible grounds for granting asylum to women. Also, the case has been made for granting asylum to women escaping repeated spousal abuse. Likewise, refugee rights lawyers working with sexually abused children have articulated the case that they should be granted asylum.

3. M. Suárez-Orozco 1999.

4. Asylum seekers can be awarded Temporary Protective Status (TPS) while their cases are being considered. This status recognizes their presence in the country, provides that they cannot be deported while their case is being considered, and allows them to work.

5. Peters 1998.

6. In Japan, for example, immigrant workers are sometimes called "3 K

workers" for the Japanese words for "dirty, demanding, and dangerous" jobs (Tsuda 1996).

7. Cornelius 1998.

8. Ibid.

9. Durand 1998.

10. L. Rodriguez 1993.

11. Chua 1999.

12. This is by far the largest cost in terms of publicly funded services of large-scale immigration. Many taxpayers who are myopic about the complexities of immigration have demonstrated increasing ambivalence in supporting the costs associated with educating immigrant children. California's controversial Proposition 187, as well as its more recent antibilingual education initiative, Proposition 227, can be seen as legal attempts to deny immigrants access to publicly funded services. (We will return to the sensitive topic of the costs associated with immigration when we discuss its myths and realities in Chapter 2.)

13. Molyneux 1999.

14. M. Suárez-Orozco 1989.

15. M. Suárez-Orozco 1994.

16. In Europe, a similar strategy has been to deem certain areas in international airports not part of the national territory—for example, parts of Zaventem airport are not technically Belgian territory but are considered to be international territory. Asylum seekers entering such airports have been turned back because they are said to remain in international territory and hence do not come under the jurisprudence of the Geneva Convention. While advanced postindustrial democracies are likely to continue to face significant numbers of asylum seekers, the greatest numbers of asylum seekers are in the developing world. For example, at the close of the millennium there were over 3 million asylum seekers in Africa.

17. In recent years there has been an explosive growth in INS detentions and deportations. According to some estimates, there are now 15,000 detainees held by the INS–60 percent of them in local jails. By the year 2001, over 24,000 men, women, and children will be held in detention centers and jails. Some 5,000 of those who are in INS detention centers today are children. According to a recent report by Humans Rights Watch: "INS detainees—including asylum seekers—are being held in jails entirely inappropriate to their noncriminal status where they may be mixed with accused and convicted criminals, and where they are sometimes subjected to physical mistreatment and grossly inadequate conditions of confinement." Human Rights Watch 1998, p. 6.

18. M. Suarez-Orozco 1989.

19. M. Suárez-Orozco and Robben 2000.

20. Zhou and Bankston 1998.

21. T. Waters 1999.

22. M. Suárez-Orozco 1989.

23. Piore 1971.

24. *New York Times,* July 13, 1999.

25. Cornelius 1986.

26. While the sojourner pattern is significant, it is important to keep in mind that today the vast majority of immigrant children settle in urban centers.

27. Basch, Schiller, and Blanc 1995.

28. M. Suárez-Orozco 1998.

29. Moya 1998.

30. Cornelius, Martin, and Hollifield 1994.

31. Ibid.

32. In Europe, the ratio of illegal immigrants to legal immigrants is a more carefully guarded secret because of its dangerous political connotations. Most hard-core right-wing political parties in Europe, including France's Front National, Belgium's Vlams Bloc, and Austria's Freedom Party, revolve around anti (illegal) immigration platforms. In the 1990s, these once-marginal parties have made substantial gains with electorates concerned about the problem of undocumented immigration.

33. We arrive at this number by extrapolating from estimates of the total number of undocumented immigrants in the United States today—roughly 10 percent of the immigrant population.

34. Human Rights Watch 1997.

35. Ibid., p. 3.

36. Eschbach, Hagan, and Rodriguez 1997.

37. See *New York Times,* February 11, 1996; June 7, 1993; July 22, 1997.

38. Hughes 1999.

39. C. Suárez-Orozco and M. Suárez-Orozco 1995.

40. *Dallas Morning News,* January 27, 1999.

41. M. Suárez-Orozco 1989.

TWO   RETHINKING IMMIGRATION

1. Note that the travails and contributions of earlier generations of Asian immigrants have been generally neglected. See for example Takaki 1989; and Hing 1993.

2. *Boston Globe,* January 11, 1996.

3. Quoted in *New York Times,* January 28, 1994.

4. Espenshade and Belanger 1998.

5. Both quotations are from *New York Times,* March 10, 1996.

6. Chavez 1992.

7. See for example, Brimelow 1995; Beck 1996; and Williamson 1996.

8. See R. Simon 1985; R. Simon and Alexander 1993.

9. Historian John Higham (1980) identifies several concerns that have historically fanned anti-immigration sentiment—anti-Catholic, anti-radical, and pro-Anglo-Saxon. Catholics were thought to be untrustworthy because of their alleged primary loyalty to the Church and the Vatican. In the case of radical immigrants (particularly those bringing with them Communist or anarchist ideas), the anxiety was over their potential threat to American capitalism and democracy. Those who opposed immigration on the basis of a pro-Anglo-Saxon stance viewed immigrants from other backgrounds as a threat to the original Anglo-Saxon cultural ethos that dominated the foundation of the Republic.

10. J. Simon 1995.

11. Quoted in R. Simon 1985, pp. 76, 88.

12. Ibid., pp. 83, 88.

13. Proposition 187, State of California, 1994.

14. Proposition 187 has faced several legal challenges (see M. Suárez-Orozco, Roos, and C. Suárez-Orozco 1999). Some observers have argued that this proposition would do nothing to prevent further undocumented immigration to California. Indeed, it could in the long term cost the taxpayers of that state far beyond whatever short-term savings could be realized by not providing public schooling to these immigrant children.

15. Some scholars have argued that the 1996 Illegal Immigration Reform and Responsibility Act will have a harmful effect on large sectors of society. The internal security provision of the new act may usher in a nationwide effort at fingerprinting, wiretapping, INS linkages with local and state law enforcement, and other measures supposedly designed to combat links between immigration, the drug trade, and terrorism. The act has obvious implications for the civil rights of immigrants and citizens alike. The new law also changes in significant ways the process by which citizens and permanent residents can bring family members to permanently reside in the United States. This feature of the law will decidedly undermine the principle of family reunification. In the late 1990s a massive law enforcement effort (which by the year 2001 will have doubled the size of the Border Patrol in just five years) was undertaken at the southern border of the United States. While illegal border crossings are more challenging and dangerous than before (resulting in a dramatic increase of migrant deaths at the border), there is little evidence that illegal immigration has been reduced. These new efforts make for dramatic symbolic politics, but they have largely failed to actually reduce illegal immigration flows through the southern sector. See Andreas 1998, pp. 345–356.

16. Cornelius, Martin, and Hollifield 1994.

17. See M. Suárez-Orozco 1994.

18. Espanshade and Belanger 1998, pp. 365–403.

19. See, for example, Huddle 1993; Borjas 1999; J. Simon 1995; Millman 1997.

20. See Borjas 1994, pp. 76–80.

21. Rice University economist Donald Huddle, in a highly publicized and controversial report, claimed that immigrants—legal and undocumented—"present in the United States in 1992 cost all levels of government that year more than $45 billion above and beyond the taxes they paid" (Huddle 1993).

22. Passel and his associates reexamined Huddle's figures and concluded that far from costing more than $45 billion, legal and undocumented immigrants nationwide contributed a net surplus of $28.7 billion. The wide discrepancies in these works suggest that the study of the fiscal implications of immigration is far from a precise science. Biases and assumptions powerfully shape these findings. See Passel 1994; Fierman 1994, pp. 67–75; and Francese 1994, pp. 85–89.

23. For example, during 1998 immigrant-owned high-technology firms in the Silicon Valley employed a total of 58,282 workers. See Saxenian 1999. In a similar vein, Fierman (1994) writes, "Compelling evidence even shows that immigrants boost overall employment on balance."

24. Mahler 1999.

25. Rothstein 1994; Francese 1994.

26. National Research Council 1997, pp. 3, 5.

27. There are important differences by state—California, for example, has been more negatively affected than other states. The study concludes that "if the net fiscal impact of all U.S. immigrant-headed households were averaged across all native households the burden would be . . . on the order of $166 to $226 per native household" (ibid., pp. 7, 8).

28. Cornelius 1993, p. 3. It is also important to note that the National Research Council's findings (1997) reveal important differences between immigrant groups: "Across the immigrant population, the size of the net fiscal burden imposed on native residents varies significantly. It is by far heaviest for households of immigrants originating in Latin America . . . These differences arise because households of Latin American immigrants tend to have lower incomes and to include more school-age children than do other immigrant households." In terms of long-term fiscal implications of immigration, it is clear that an important issue will be the educational adaptation of the children of today's immigrants: more education today means less fiscal burden down the road.

29. It is interesting to note that whereas in the United States "competi-

tion" is generally seen in positive terms (especially when it comes to economic competition), with immigration the connotation seems to produce a negative aftertaste (National Research Council 1997, quote on p. 6).

30. Research on the effects of immigrant workers on the wages of American workers illustrates the difficulties in separating those changes generated by immigration from those changes generated by an increasingly transnational capitalism. While some claim that it is large-scale immigration that has negatively influenced the wages of some American workers, others suggest that it is actually the global economy that is the primary culprit for the decline. This distinction, however, is somewhat academic because immigration flows today are directly related to global economic changes.

31. Cornelius 1993.

32. Papademetriou 1994, pp. 1–5.

33. Sociologist Roger Waldinger (1997b) has argued that immigrant networks have generated new hiring practices whereby bosses come to rely on their immigrant workers for further hires. Waldinger argues that although these immigrant hiring networks are highly efficient, in the Los Angeles area they generate forms of "social closure" that tend to exclude nonimmigrant workers, particularly African Americans.

34. The NRC report indicates that these networks do not appear to be a nationwide phenomenon. See National Research Council 1997, p. 5.

35. Borjas 1999. It is important to highlight that the portion of the U.S. economy that is affected by immigration is rather small; the total size of the U.S. economy is 7 trillion dollars, and immigrant-related economic activities are a minuscule portion of that total. (Recall that the NRC suggests that the gain related to immigration is between one to ten billion dollars). Immigrants will neither "make" nor "break" the U.S. economy.

36. Quoted in Rohter 1993, p. 4.

37. See, for example, a *60 Minutes* story aired on January 23, 1994.

38. See Simon 1995. A 1993 survey of 241 non-English speakers living in a migrant camp found that 75.5 percent of the residents had never used "Medi-Cal" (Eisenstadt and Thorup 1994).

39. See National Research Council 1998; Earls 1998; and Simon 1995.

40. See National Research Council 1998. There are several possible explanations for this phenomenon. One is that immigrants simply self-elect; only the healthier members of a population are likely to migrate. A second interpretation is that once settled in the new land, immigrants organize their own traditional or folk medical practices, therefore bypassing the medical institutions of the host society. Yet another possibility, which is especially likely for those living near the border areas, is that they simply return home when in need of health care.

41. The researchers used the 1996 March Current Population Survey and the National Health Survey.

42. Clearly, health insurance provides essential access to care. Brown and his colleagues found that noncitizen children are three times as likely as citizen children to lack health insurance. Even more worrisome, noncitizen children are at greater risk of lacking health insurance regardless of their length of stay in the United States. Brown et al. 1998.

43. See Eisenstadt and Thorup 1994.

44. See Brown et al. 1998; Hayes-Bautista et al. 1988; and ibid.

45. J. Simon 1995.

46. Espenshade and Belanger 1998.

47. Chavez 1992.

48. Nelan 1993, p. 11.

49. Wolf 1988, p. 2.

50. Quoted in Chavez 1992, p. 16.

51. The highly visible participation of immigrants in the World Trade Center bombing in New York as well as in other terrorist plots heightens that anxiety. It is important to keep in perspective however, that the participation of immigrants in such terrorist acts is statistically insignificant.

52. Allport 1979.

53. See Wolf 1988.

54. Unauthorized crossings used to be mostly acts of self-smuggling. More recently, however, immigrants making such crossings have increasingly relied on the work of professional alien smugglers and document forgers—a high-profit growth industry on both sides of the border. Because immigrants now try to cross the border at more difficult points of entry, the price of being smuggled has also gone up—the price of being smuggled from Tijuana to Los Angeles doubled from 1994 to 1996. See Andreas 1998.

55. Wolf 1988, quote on p. 23.

56. T. Waters 1999.

57. J. Simon 1989, p. 304.

58. Eisenstadt and Thorup 1994.

59. See T. Waters 1999.

60. Borjas 1999.

61. Brimelow 1995.

62. See, for example, Higham 1980 for a classic study of the history and characteristics of U.S. anti-immigrant sentiment.

63. Political observers have noted that it was probably this display of Mexican flags that led many initially neutral voters to cast their ballot in favor of the controversial proposition.

64. Beriss 1996; M. Suárez-Orozco 1996.

65. M. Waters 1990.

66. Gutierrez 1998.

67. M. Waters 1990.

68. Quoted in Portes and Schauffler 1994, p. 640.

69. See, inter alia, ibid.; Portes and Hao 1998; *Boston Globe,* July 13, 1997.

70. Sachs 1999, p. 6. in considering these data, however, it is important to keep two points in mind. First, these are self-reported data and not an independent assessment of the respondent's English language skills. Furthermore, casual fluency may not be adequate to compete for higher-level jobs.

71. Portes and Schauffler 1994.

72. Spanish speakers are more likely than Chinese-speaking children to value continuing to speak their native language. A little over a quarter of the Chinese children indicated that maintaining their home language was *not* important.

73. Portes and Hao 1998.

74. See for example, National Research Council 1998.

75. In the words of immigration historian David Gutierrez (1998), "Demographic shifts of this magnitude have contributed to an expansion of an ethnic Mexican and Latino regional economic, social, and cultural infrastructure that dwarfs that which evolved earlier in the century." For an elegant study of the transformation of Miami through immigration, see Portes and Stepick 1993.

76. Geertz 1973.

77. Ainslie 1998.

78. Johnson 1997.

79. Wagner and Venezky 1999.

80. Snow 1997.

81. See *New York Times,* April 26, 1997.

82. See *New York Times,* July 23, 1999. Of course not all of these foreign-born physics graduate students are immigrants—some will indeed return to their countries of birth, while others will surely go on to have productive scientific careers in the United States.

83. See Saxenian 1999. We are thankful to Professor Michael Jones-Correa of the Department of Government at Harvard University for alerting us to this important new study.

84. See for example, Borjas 1995.

85. Edmonston and Passel 1994, p. 41.

86. Their children (and their children's children) would return to the "old country" to search for their roots.

87. See, for example, Gans 1999; Portes 1997, pp. 799–825.

88. Levitt 1997; Basch, Schiller, and Blanc 1995; Guarnizo, 1994, pp. 70–86; Portes 1996b.

89. Basch, Schiller, and Blanc 1995.

90. Levitt 1996.

91. Portes 1998, pp. 1–20.

92. See Moya 1998.

93. O'Neill 1984. Language schools are not a new phenomenon: German, Hebrew, and Japanese schools were quite popular in earlier eras of immigration.

94. Another problem is that the term transnationalism often means different things to different people. Some use the term to refer to the immigrants' shuttling back and forth between their old and new countries. Others seem to pay less attention to the back and forth issue and concentrate on how immigrant segregation—definitely not a new phenomenon—generates cultural models and social practices that seem to separate new immigrants from mainstream culture and society. Still others use transnationalism to mean nearly anything relating to immigration or to global capitalism and global culture.

95. Of the children in our sample, 93 percent keep in touch with those back home either by phone, telephone, audiotape, videotape, or a combination of methods.

96. In fact, we found a paradoxical outcome among those children who did engage with these new technologies: the technologies themselves helped immigrant children acquire English language skills. As they interacted with other children around issues of common interest such as computer games and popular culture, they became more oriented to the "mainstream."

97. Sanger reports that Asian Americans tend to have more access to the internet and use it more often than Latinos and African Americans. See Sanger 1999.

98. See for example, Higham 1975.

99. See Waldinger and Bozorgmehr 1996.

100. See for example, Portes 1996a, pp. 1–15.

101. See Myers 1998, p. 188.

102. See Murnane 1996.

103. Waldinger and Bozorgmehr 1996.

104. Orfield 1998.

105. Portes 1996a, pp. 72–73.

106. Friedman 1999.

107. Romanucci-Ross and De Vos 1995.

THREE THE PSYCHOSOCIAL EXPERIENCE OF IMMIGRATION

1. Garcia-Coll and Magnuson 1998.

2. In 1996, 915,900 immigrants were formally admitted to the United States. Among them, 596,264 were family-sponsored immigrants—most of

them the children and spouses of those already here. Likewise, in Europe family reunification is one of the few formal ways to migrate to the continent.

3. M. Waters 1999.

4. Danticat 1994, p. 51.

5. Ibid., p. 49.

6. Schlossberg 1984.

7. Dohrenwend 1986.

8. House 1974, pp. 12–27.

9. Falicov 1998.

10. See Ainslie 1998; L. Grinberg and R. Grinberg 1989.

11. Somach 1995.

12. See Horowitz 1986; Smajkic and Weane 1995.

13. M. Suárez-Orozco 1989.

14. Eschbach, Hagan, and Rodriguez 1997; Amnesty International 1998, p. 24.

15. All quotations from our informants are translations from their native languages.

16. Orfield 1998.

17. Sluzki 1979, pp. 379–390.

18. Ainslie 1998; Arrendondo-Dowd 1981, pp. 376–378; L. Grinberg and R. Grinberg 1989; Rumbaut 1977; Sluzki 1979; M. Suárez-Orozco 1998.

19. Volkan 1993, pp. 63–69. For a brilliant analysis of the psychodynamics of loss among immigrants, see Ainslie 1998.

20. L. Grinberg and R. Grinberg 1989.

21. Ibid.

22. See Berry 1998; Flaskerud and Uman 1996, pp. 123–133; J. F. Smart and D. W. Smart 1995, pp. 390–396.

23. Hoffmann 1989, p. 151.

24. Orfield and Yun 1999.

25. M. Suárez-Orozco 1998.

26. Falicov 1998.

27. Wong-Fillmore 1991, pp. 323–346.

28. Santiago 1998, p. 18.

29. Sluzki 1979; Falicov 1998.

30. Athey and Ahearn 1991.

31. Vigil 1988.

32. Cao 1997, p. 35.

33. Shuval 1980.

34. Hoffman 1989, p. 159.

35. Urrea 1998, p. 41.

36. Hoffman 1989, p. 128.

37. Ibid., p. 145.
38. *New York Daily News,* April 1, 1999.
39. See *American Behavioral Scientist* 1999.
40. Espin 1987, esp. p. 493.
41. Hondagneu-Sotelo 1994.
42. Min 1998.
43. Santiago 1998, pp. 12 and 25.
44. Espin 1999; Olsen 1998.
45. Goodenow and Espin 1993, pp. 173–184.
46. Olsen 1988.
47. Valenzuela 1999, pp. 720–742; Waters 1997; Smith 1999.
48. Valenzuela 1999.
49. Vigil 1988; Smith 1999.
50. Smith 1999.
51. Khoury et al. 1999, pp. 21–40.
52. Hernandez and Charney 1998.
53. Olneck and Lazerson 1974, pp. 453–482.
54. Brandon 1991, pp. 45–61.
55. Waters 1997.
56. Gibson 1997, pp. 431–454.
57. Olsen 1998.
58. Ibid., p. 125.
59. Ibid.
60. De Vos 1992a; De Vos 1992b; Ogbu and Simons 1998, pp. 155–188.
61. Gibson 1997.
62. See Earls 1997.
63. Fordham 1996; Gibson 1988; Smith 1999; Waters 1996.
64. Falicov 1998; J. F. Smart and D. W. Smart 1995.
65. Earls 1997.
66. Flaskerud and Uman 1996; C. Suárez-Orozco 1998.
67. Garcia-Coll and Magnuson 1998; Laosa 1989; Rumbaut 1997.
68. Shuval 1980.
69. Garcia-Coll and Magnuson 1998; ibid.
70. Wheaton 1983, pp. 208–229.
71. Lazarus and Folkman 1984; Pearlin and Schooler 1978, pp. 2–21.
72. Cobb 1988, pp. 300–314; Cohen and Syme 1985.
73. Wills 1985.
74. Heller and Swindle 1983.
75. Chavez 1992; J. F. Smart and D. W. Smart 1995.
76. Waldinger 1997b; Cornelius 1998.
77. Orfield and Yun 1999.
78. School authorities and news reports substantiated this finding. Alex

Stepick and his team of researchers at Florida International University are currently doing important research on violence and immigrant children in American schools.

79. Garcia-Coll and Magnuson 1998, p. 119; Adams 1990.

80. Adams 1990.

FOUR REMAKING IDENTITIES

1. C. Suárez-Orozco and M. Suárez-Orozco 1995.

2. Hoffman 1989, p. 127.

3. Alvarez 1992, pp. 108–109.

4. Hoffman 1989, p. 146.

5. Ibid., p. 159.

6. Proulx 1996, p. 32.

7. Steinberg, Brown, and Dornbusch 1996, p. 98. Steinberg argues that the current American adolescent peer culture is in many ways corrosive. The peer culture actively demeans academic success and disparages students who attempt to do well in school. Widespread cheating and active avoidance of assignments and homework are the norm. In his discussion of both Asian and Latino immigrant students, Steinberg found a rapid decline in performance with increased length of exposure to the American peer culture. Given that it is based on a carefully constructed, large-scale study of 20,000 American students from nine urban, suburban, and rural high schools and confirms a number of findings from other studies, his conclusion is hard to ignore.

8. Princeton sociologist Alejandro Portes (1996a) has used the term "rainbow underclass" to describe this phenomenon.

9. According to Erikson (1963), the sense of identity is one of personal sameness and historical continuity. In Erikson's developmental model, during adolescence youth go through various stages of exploration that eventually result in a commitment to identity. Marcia (1980) has elaborated upon Erikson's stages. In Marcia's model, youth undergo a stage of "diffused identity" when they are not engaged in identity exploration. They may move into a phase of "foreclosure," when identity is largely based on either on parental values or what is mirrored back by others in the society. During a phase of "moratorium," the youth explores alternative identity pathways and is often confused about which to follow. The final stage in this unilineal developmental model is that of "achieved identity"—when the youngster makes a firm commitment and develops a clear understanding of his or her own identity.

10. See Kagan, Appiah, and Noam 1998; Phinney 1998.

11. See L. Grinberg and R. Grinberg 1989; Vigil 1988.

12. Stonequist 1937, p. 4.

13. Anthropologists, however, have noted that class stratification is a relatively recent phenomenon. Historically, human systems of stratification have been organized around inequalities based upon age (e.g., the gerentocratic systems of Highland New Guinea) or gender (e.g., the patriarchal systems in the pastoral Middle East and Africa).

14. De Vos and Suárez-Orozco 1990.

15. See, for example, Freire 1995.

16. De Vos 1973; De Vos 1980; De Vos and Suárez-Orozco 1990; Ogbu 1974; Ogbu 1978; Ogbu and Matute-Bianchi; Gibson and Ogbu 1991; Fordham and Ogbu 1986; Fordham 1996; Jacob and Jordan 1987.

17. De Vos and Suárez-Orozco 1990.

18. Espenshade and Belanger 1998.

19. De Vos and Suárez-Orozco 1990.

20. For example, when high-achieving African American university students are told before taking an exam that the exam has proven to differentiate between blacks and whites (in favor of whites) the performance of the African American students goes down. Likewise, when women are told that the test they are about to take differentiates between men and women (in favor of men), the women's scores go down. In both cases, when African American students and women students are not told that the test they are about to take differentiates between groups, their performance is significantly better (Steele 1997a, 1997b; quote on 1997a, p. 614).

21. Fuligini 1997; Kao and Tienda 1995; Portes and Zhou 1993; Rumbaut 1996a; Steinberg, Brown, and Dornbusch 1996; C. Suárez-Orozco and M. Suárez-Orozco 1995.

22. Winnicott (1971) argued that "the mother functions as a mirror, providing the infant with a precise reflection of his own experience and gestures, despite their fragmented and formless qualities. 'When I look I am seen, so I exist."

23. Imperfections in the reflected rendition mar and inhibit the child's capacity for self-experience and integration and interfere with the process of "personalization." The infant is highly dependent upon the reflection of the experience she receives from her mothering figure. The mother provides clues about the environment. In determining whether she need be frightened by new stimuli, the infant will first look to her mother's expression and response. An expression of interest or calm will reassure the infant, while an expression of concern will alarm her. Even more crucial is the mother's response to the infant's actions. Does the mother show delight when the infant reaches for an object, or does she ignore it or show disapproval? No one response (or non-response) is likely to have much affect but the accumulation of experiences is significant in the formation of the child's identities and sense of self-worth. A child whose accomplishments

are mirrored favorably is likely to feel more valuable than the child whose accomplishments are either largely ignored or worse still, denigrated. Although mirroring (along with a number of his other concepts) is an important contribution to our understanding of the developing child, Winnicott—like many of his psychoanalytic colleagues—overlooks the powerful forces of social systems and culture in shaping personal relationships.

24. Takaki 1989. In a less benign example of "false good" mirroring, individuals who are surrounded by those who do not give them negative feedback and laud even minimal accomplishments may develop a distorted view of their own abilities and achievements. This is sometimes the case with political leaders or movie stars as well as others with power and influence. There is also recent evidence that some children are over praised; the resulting inflated sense of self-worth coupled with a low tolerance for frustration may be partially linked to violent outbursts. See Seligman 1998.

25. Rosenthal and Jacobson 1968.

26. Du Bois 1986, pp. 364–365.

27. Taylor 1994.

28. Santiago 1998, pp. 88, 84

29. Social psychologist Martin Seligman has contributed much to our understanding of optimism and pessimism. He notes: "The defining characteristic of pessimists is that they tend to believe that bad events will last a long time, will undermine everything they do, and are their own fault. The optimists, who are confronted with the same hard knocks of this world, think about misfortune in the opposite way. They tend to believe defeat is just a temporary setback, that its causes are confined to this one case. The optimists believe defeat is not their fault; Circumstances, bad luck, or other people brought it about. Such people are unfazed by defeat. Confronted by a bad situation, they perceive it as a challenge to try harder" (Seligman 1990, pages 4–5). Seligman maintains that hope is the single most important characteristic of optimism.

30. Navarette 1993.

31. Ibid., p. 60.

32. Fordham and Ogbu 1986.

33. Rodriguez 1982.

34. De Vos 1992b.

35. Portes 1993, p. 2.

36. Fordham and Ogbu 1986.

37. Navarette 1993, p. 260.

38. Villareal 1959, pp. 149–150.

39. Vigil 1988, p. 6.

40. Ibid.

41. L. Rodriguez 1993, p. 134.

42. Stonequist 1937, p. 15.

43. This case study is taken from field work conducted in the early 1980s in the San Francisco area.

44. Phinney 1990. Max Weber typifies the approach of defining ethnic groups by focusing on the existence of a cultural system. For Weber, an ethnic group consists of those "human groups that entertain a subjective belief in their common descent because of similarities of physical type or customs or both, or because of the memories of colonization or migration" (Weber 1968). Other researchers have emphasized the active crafting and self-selection of specific social or cultural markers to delineate ethnic boundaries and ethnic identities (Barth 1969). The markers can be "objective" (such as language, religion, choices of dress, music, and food) or "subjective" (a feeling of commitment or belonging to the group, shared values, and so forth). From our theoretical perspective, in the remaking of ethnic groupings in the context of large-scale immigration, the issue of race and color seems to powerfully limit the ways that new arrivals can define themselves. Immigrants of color entering racial and ethnically stratified societies are very likely to, in the long term, be forced into the preexisting local racial categories above all other markers (M. Waters 1999). Note that Roosens (1989) argues that a narrow focus on objective markers overlooks the saliency of subjective markers.

45. Janet Helms (1990) uses a definition of "racial identity" quite similar to our definition of ethnic identity. She claims that racial identity is "a sense of group or collective identity based on one's *perception* that he or she shares a common racial heritage with a particular racial group."

46. Romanucci-Ross and De Vos 1995.

47. Triandis (1989) argues that identity arises out of an interaction between the individual (intrapsychic self-perceptions) and two dimensions of the social environment, which he has termed the "collective" and the "public." The collective encompass the perceptions that one has about one's own group and is born out of a collective history, language, and social practices. The public is how the dominant group views the ethnic group–the "social mirror." Other scholars have argued that in plural societies ethnic identity can be strongly or weakly imposed upon the ethnic group by the dominant group. Independently, both in situations where ethnicity is strongly or weakly imposed from the outside, ethnic group members may strongly identify with and organize their lives around their ethnic identities (Cornell and Hartmann 1998).

48. Deany, Kay 1996; Taylor 1994.

49. See Marcia 1966 and Phinney 1998. In addition, William Cross (1978) has proposed an influential model to describe a stage-wise process

in which African Americans explore their racial identity in a racially stratified society.

50. Parham 1989; Tatum 1992; Tatum 1997.

51. Other theorists do view the process as linear and evolutionary— from least to most mature (see Cross 1991; Marcia 1966; and Phinney 1998.)

52. Historically, ethnicity becomes most salient under conditions of perceived threat and attack from the outside. The moving film *The Garden of the Finzi-Contini's* portrays beautifully the plight of "fully assimilated" upper-status Italian Jews who simply could not believe that their ethnic and racial background would doom them in their beloved Italy. It is not until the very climax of the film that they discover that they are first and foremost Jews and that their Italian sense of self was irrelevant in the context of the genocidal practices of the Fascist Italian regime.

53. M. Waters 1999, quote from p. 6.

54. Ibid., p. 164.

55. Ibid., p. 169.

56. In the era of AIDS, however, this strategy can be a double-edged sword for Haitians. According to anthropologist Alex Stepick (1998), many Haitian children in Miami, much to their parents' dismay, disavowed their Haitian origins in order to escape the stigma that Haitians are "AIDS carriers."

57. Zéphir 1996, pp. 52–53. Renowned Stanford psychologist Claude Steele has also identified a similar strategy used by upper-status African American men to actively distance themselves from African American men from the underclass. To appear less threatening to whites they pass in the street, they may be heard to "whistle Vivaldi." By doing so the men are consciously sending off cues to the social audience that they are cultured and therefore not threatening (Steele 1997b).

58. Quotation from M. Waters 1999, p. 8. Waters notes that West Indian immigrants tend to have a different attitude toward employment and work than do many native born African Americans of similar socioeconomic backgrounds. She argues that employers view them as greatly valuing the opportunity to work, willing to work very hard, and not being resentful of service occupations (which native-born African Americas frequently feel uncomfortable and ambivalent about given the slavery legacy). She comments that West Indian immigrants tend to be highly ambitious and maintain an "achievement ideology" (M. Waters 1999, p. 159). Furthermore, "low anticipation of sour race relations allow them to have better interpersonal interactions with white Americans than many native African Americans" (p. 7). As a result they tend to have better day-to-day interactions and pay less "attention to racialism" (p. 8). At the same time they tend to be mil-

itant in naming and combatting overt discrimination. She also notes that West Indian immigrants tend to place a high value on education.

FIVE   THE CHILDREN OF IMMIGRATION IN SCHOOL

1. Tyler, Murnane, and Levy 1995.

2. Harvard sociologist Mary Waters (1997) points out that prior to the 1950s, first- and second-generation Polish and Italian immigrants usually only received an elementary-school education. She notes that at the beginning of the twentieth century, fewer than 30 percent of German immigrants and fewer than 25 percent of Italian immigrants stayed in school past the sixth grade.

3. C. Suárez-Orozco and M. Suárez-Orozco 1995.

4. Ibid.

5. This comment was *not* made by a superintendent of a school district participating in the Longitudinal Immigrant Student Adaptation study.

6. Olsen 1988, p. 75.

7. Ibid.

8. Orfield and Yun (1999) found that the typical school attended by the average Asian-origin student is 47 percent white. On the other hand, Latino-origin students attend the most highly segregated schools of any group in the United States today. In 1996, only 25 percent of Latino students attended majority white schools.

9. So that they can afford their living quarters, it is not uncommon for newly arrived families to share a small housing unit with other close relatives and friends. Many of our informants live in households with more than one nuclear family. It is not uncommon for two or three families to pool resources.

10. Orfield 1998.

11. Wilson 1997.

12. Massey and Denton 1993.

13. De Vos 1992b.

14. Earls 1997.

15. Zhou forthcoming.

16. August & Hakuta 1997; Carter and Chatfield 1986; Lucas 1990.

17. An ethnographic study of a large number of immigrant schools in Miami found that three factors were consistently present in schools with "cultures of violence." First, school officials tended to deny that the school had problems with violence or drugs. Second, many of the school staff members exhibited "non-caring" behaviors toward the students. Third, the schools' security measures were lax. (Collier 1998).

18. Orfield and Yun 1999, p. 22.

19. Orfield and Yun have found that Asians "on average, experience a

high degree of integration with groups of students who tend to have higher average achievement levels and less linguistic isolation. There are stark differences, however, within the Asian population. Asians who lived in this country prior to the end of the Vietnam War tended to be wealthier and more educated than the large refugee groups who arrived after the war. So, while the average Asian faces a much more integrated picture than the average Black or Latino student, there are large numbers of Asian students who live in very segregated poverty situations. Asian segregation in the nation is growing significantly" (ibid., page 16).

20. Orfield et al. 1999.

21. Lieberson, Dalto, and Johnson 1975. See also Portes and Hao 1998.

22. Ana Celia Zentella (1997) has demonstrated that rather than "failing for words," code switchers may use this linguistic strategy as an act of ethnic solidarity. She maintains that code switching requires understanding the rules of both languages.

23. Snow 1993.

24. Ibid.

25. Ibid.

26. Ibid. See also August and Hakuta 1997.

27. August and Hakuta 1997, p. 28.

28. Snow 1997, p. 31.

29. August and Hakuta 1997.

30. Sommer 1999.

31. August and Hakuta 1997.

32. Cited in Crawford 1991, p. 32.

33. Snow 1997.

34. First and Carrera 1988.

35. Ibid., quote on p. 110.

36. Ibid.

37. Ibid., and Snow 1993.

38. Snow 1993.

39. For every native speaker of English, there are three non-native speakers of English (Kachru 1994).

40. August and Hakuta 1997.

41. Valdéz 1998.

41. Donato, Menchaca, and Valencia 1991.

42. Not being in a bilingual program can also place immigrant children at risk. Some studies have found that children who are not in bilingual programs are at greater danger of dropping out than those who are (see Padilla et al. 1991).

43. This is especially true for children learning to read. Research strongly suggests that it is important not to teach a young child to read in a

second language before she has firmly mastered reading in her first. Because learning to read requires matching sounds to letters, phonemic decoding optimally occurs in the language the child is most familiar with. Once she has mastered reading in her native language, she can transfer her reading skills to the new language (Snow 1993).

44. While many condemned Proposition 227 as yet another xenophobic anti-immigrant initiative, large numbers of immigrant parents supported the proposition.

45. See Gándara 1994. See also M. Suárez-Orozco, Roos, and C. Suárez-Orozco 1999.

46. See Minicucci and Olsen 1992; Heubert 1999.

47. Some districts, aware that immigrant students do not do as well on such tests, opt not to include their performance on final reports.

48. M. Suárez-Orozco, Roos, and C. Suárez-Orozco 1999.

49. Ibid.

50. Valdéz 1998.

51. See Vigotsky 1978; Tharp and Gallimore 1988; Huerta 1998; Dalton 1998; Moll 1988; Nieto 1996; Trueba 1989.

52. Valdéz 1998, p. 7.

53. Family characteristics have a powerful effect on the schooling achievement of children. In a classic study, James Coleman and his colleagues (1966) found that parental socioeconomic status has a greater effect on a child's school achievement than any other variable. A number of other studies have also examined the connections between parents and school achievement among immigrant children. See, for example, Zhou and Bankston 1998; Gándara 1995; Delgado-Gaitan and Trueba 1991; and Garcia-Coll, Surrey, and Weingarten 1998.

54. Camus 1995, p. 321.

EPILOGUE

1. For recent policy and economic perspectives on the new immigration, see for example, Borjas 1999; Millman 1997; and Beck 1996.

2. A number of observers of the new immigration have noted that there is dissonance between immigration policy (e.g., how many immigrants do we allow to enter the country each year?) and what may be called integration policies (e.g., how do we best educate the large numbers of immigrant children already here?). Part of the problem lies in the fact that immigration policy is set by the federal government, while integration policies are left for state, county, and city governments to decide.

3. For a comprehensive overview of the social science scholarship on the children of immigrants, see Portes and Zhou 1993, pp. 63–95. See also Rumbaut and Cornelius 1995.

4. The tax revolt originated with Proposition 13 in California—paradoxically the state with the largest number of new immigrants.

5. Learning English is hard and it is magical thinking to demand that young students master it in a year. In the area of language learning, time and exposure are of the essence.

6. Nevertheless, the majority of psychological studies of acculturation use knowledge of English as the stand-in variable for acculturation.

7. Portes 1996a.

8. Massey and Denton 1993.

9. For an overview of recent research on immigration and family ties, see Rumbaut 1996b. See also C. Suárez-Orozco and M. Suárez-Orozco 1995, and Falicov 1998. For an overview of immigrant optimism and achievement orientation, see Kao and Tienda 1995, pp. 1–19.

10. We concur with Teresa LaFromboise and her colleagues (1998) on the need to reconceptualize what they call the "linear model of cultural acquisition."

11. Margaret Gibson (1988) articulates a sophisticated theoretical argument on immigrant transculturation and a calculated strategy of "accommodation without assimilation" in her study of highly successful Sikh immigrants in California. For a theoretical statement on the psychology of ethnic identity and cultural pluralism, see Phinney 1998.

12. Much of the thinking about acculturation was developed to address earlier transatlantic waves of European immigration. The immigrants then were different (largely Europeans); the country was different (on the eve of the industrial expansion where immigrant workers and consumers became key players); and the world was different (more neatly bounded into national spaces).

13. See, for example, Glazer and Moynihan 1970.

14. Handlin 1951.

REFERENCES

Adams, P. L. 1990. "Prejudice and Exclusion as Social Trauma." In J. D. Noshpitz and R. D. Coddington, eds., *Stressors and Adjustment Disorders*. New York: John Wiley and Sons.

Ahearn, Jr., Frederick L., and Jean L. Athey. 1991. *Refugee Children: Theory, Research, and Services*. Baltimore, Md.: Johns Hopkins University Press.

Ainslie, Ricardo. 1998. "Cultural Mourning, Immigration, and Engagement: Vignettes from the Mexican Experience." In Marcelo M. Suárez-Orozco, ed., *Crossings: Mexican Immigration in Interdisciplinary Perspectives*. Cambridge, Mass.: David Rockefeller Center for Latin American Studies and Harvard University Press.

Alba, Richard, and Victor Nee. 1997. "Rethinking Assimilation Theory for a New Era of Immigration." *International Migration Review* 31: 826–874.

Allport, Gordon. 1979. *The Nature of Prejudice*. Reading, Mass.: Addison-Wesley.

Alvarez, Julia. 1992. *How the Garcia Girls Lost Their Accents*. New York: Plume.

American Behavioral Scientist. 1999. Issue devoted to "Gender and Contemporary U.S. Immigration" 42, no. 4.

Amnesty International. 1998. "From San Diego to Brownsville: Human Rights Violations on the USA-Mexico Border." *New Release*, May 20, 24.

Andreas, Peter. 1998. "The U.S. Immigration Control Offensive: Constructing an Image of Order on the Southwest Border." In Marcelo M. Suárez-Orozco, ed., *Crossings: Mexican Immigration in Interdisciplinary Perspectives*. Cambridge, Mass.: David Rockefeller Center for Latin American Studies and Harvard University Press, pp. 343–356.

Arrendondo-Dowd, P. 1981. "Personal Loss and Grief as a Result of Immigration." *Personnel and Guidance Journal* 59: 376–378.

August, Diane, and Kenji Hakuta. 1997. *Improving Schooling for Language-Minority Children: A Research Agenda.* Washington, D.C.: National Academy Press.

Barth, Frederik. 1969. *Ethnic Groups and Boundaries: The Social Organization of Culture Difference.* Boston: Little, Brown.

Basch, L., N. G. Schiller, and C. S. Blanc. 1995. *Nations Unbound: Transnational Projects, Postcolonial Predicaments and Deterritorialized Nation-States.* Basel, Switz.: Gordon and Breach.

Beck, Roy. 1996. *The Case against Immigration: The Moral, Economic, Social, and Environmental Reasons for Reducing U.S. Immigration Back to Traditional Levels.* New York: Norton.

Beriss, David. 1996. "Scarves, Schools, and Segregation: The Foulard Affair." In Anne Corbett and Bob Moon, eds., *Education in France: Continuity and Change in the Mitterand Years, 1981–1995.* London: Routledge.

Berry, John W. 1998. "Psychology of Acculturation." In Nancy Goldenberg and Judy B. Veroff, eds., *The Culture and Psychology Reader.* New York: New York University Press, 1998.

Booth, Alan, Ann C. Crouter, and Nancy Landale, eds. 1996. *Immigration and the Family: Research and Policy on U.S. Immigrants.* Mahwah, N.J.: Lawrence Erlbaum.

Borjas, George. 1994. "Tired, Poor, on Welfare." In N. Mills, ed., *Arguing Immigration.* New York: Simon and Schuster, pp. 76–80.

——— 1995. "Assimilation in Cohort Quality Revisited: What Happened to Immigrant Earnings in the 1980s?" *Journal of Labor Economics* 13, no. 2: 211–245.

——— 1999. *Heaven's Door: Immigration Policy and the American Economy.* Princeton, N.J.: Princeton University Press.

Brandon, P. 1991. "Gender Differences in Young Asian Americans' Educational Attainment." *Sex Roles* 25, nos. 1/2: 45–61.

Brimelow, Peter. 1995. *Alien Nation: Common Sense about America's Immigration Disaster.* New York: Random House.

Brown, Richard, Roberta Wyn, Hongjian Yu, Abel Valenzuela, and Liane Dong. 1998. "Access to Health Insurance and Health Care for Mexican American Children in Immigrant Families." In Marcelo M. Suárez-Orozco, ed., , pp. 225–247.

Camus, Albert. 1995. *The First Man.* New York: Alfred Knopf.

Cao, Lan. 1997. *Monkey Bridge.* New York: Penguin.

Carter, T., and M. Chatfield. 1986. "Effective Bilingual Schools: Implications for Policy and Practice." *American Journal of Education* 95: 200–232.

Chavez, Leo R. 1992. *Shadowed Lives: Undocumented Immigrants in American Society.* Fort Worth, Tex.: Harcourt Brace.

Christenfeld, Timothy. 1996. "The World: Alien Expressions; Wretched Refuse Is Just the Start." *New York Times,* March 10.

Chua, Lee Beng. 1999. "Uprooting and Replanting: Making and Remaking Meanings of Achievement." Ed.D. diss., Harvard University Graduate School of Education.

Cobb, S. 1988. "Social Support as a Moderator of Life Stress." *Psychosomatic Medicine* 3, no. 5: 300–314.

Cohen, S., and S. L. Syme. 1985. "Issues in the Study and Application of Social Support." In S. Cohen and S. L. Syme, eds., *Social Support and Health.* Orlando, Fla.: Academic Press.

Coleman, J., et al. 1966. *Equality and Educational Opportunity.* Washington, D.C.: U.S. Government Printing Office.

Collier, Michael. 1998. "Cultures of Violence in Miami-Dade Public Schools." Working Paper of the Immigration and Ethnicity Institute, Florida International University.

Cornelius, Wayne A. 1986. *From Sojourners to Settlers: The Changing Profile of Mexican Migration to the United States.* Stanford, Calif.: Americas Program, Stanford University.

——— 1993. "Neo-Nativists Feed on Myopic Fears." *Los Angeles Times,* July 12, p. 3.

——— 1998. "The Structural Embeddedness of Demand for Mexican Immigrant Labor," in Marcelo M. Suárez-Orozco, ed., *Crossings: Mexican Immigration in Interdisciplinary Perspectives.* Cambridge, Mass.: David Rockefeller Center for Latin American Studies and Harvard University Press, pp. 113–155.

Cornelius, Wayne A., Philip L. Martin, and James F. Hollifield. 1994. *Controlling Immigration: A Global Perspective.* Stanford, Calif.: Stanford University Press.

Cornell, Stephen, and Douglas Hartmann. 1998. *Ethnicity and Race: Making Identities in a Changing World.* Thousand Oaks, Calif.: Pine Forge Press.

Crawford, James. 1991. *Bilingual Education: History, Politics, Theory, and Practice. 2d ed.* Los Angeles, Calif.: Bilingual Educational Services.

Cross, William. 1978. "The Thomas and Cross Models of Psychological Nigrescence: A Literature Review." *Journal of Black Psychology* 4: 13–31.

——— 1991. *Shades of Black.* Philadelphia: Temple University Press.

Dalton, S. 1998. *Pedagogy Matters: Standards for Effective Teaching Practice.* Santa Cruz: Center for Research on Education and Diversity, University of California.

Danticat, Edwidge. 1994. *Breath, Eyes, Memory.* New York: Vintage Press.

Deany, Kay. 1996. "Social Identification." In E. T. Higgins and A. W. Kruglanski, eds., *Social Psychology: Handbook of Basic Principles.* New York: Guilford Press.

Delgado-Gaitan, C., and Henry Trueba. 1991. *Crossing Cultural Borders.* London: Falmer.

DePalma, Anthony. 1999. "Low Pay and Hard Work, Blessed by Immigration." *New York Times,* July 13, p. A5.

De Vos, George. 1973. *Socialization for Achievement: Essays on the Cultural Psychology of the Japanese.* Berkeley: University of California Press.

——— 1980. "Ethnic Adaptation and Minority Status." *Journal of Cross— Cultural Psychology* 11, no. 1: 101–125.

——— 1992a. "The Passing of Passing." In George De Vos, *Social Cohesion and Alienation: Minorities in the United States and Japan.* Boulder, Colo.: Westview.

——— 1992b. *Social Cohesion and Alienation: Minorities in the United States and Japan.* Boulder, Colo.: Westview.

De Vos, George, and Marcelo M. Suárez-Orozco. 1990. *Status Inequality: The Self in Culture.* Newbury Park, Calif.: Sage.

Dohrenwend, B. P. 1986. "Theoretical Formulation of Life Stress Variables." In A. Eichler, M. M. Silverman, and D. M. Pratt, eds., *How to Define and Research Stress.* Washington, D.C.: American Psychiatric Press.

Donato, R., Martha Menchaca, and Richard Valencia. 1991. "Segregation, Desegregation, and Integration of Chicano Students: Problems and Prospects." In Richard Valencia, ed., *Chicano School Failure and Success: Research and Policy for the 1990s.* London: Falmer.

Du Bois, W. E. B. 1986. "The Souls of Black Folk." In Nathan Huggins, ed., *W. E. B. Du Bois: Writings.* New York: Library of America.

Durand, Jorge. 1998. "Migration and Integration." In Marcelo M. Suárez-Orozco, ed., *Crossings: Mexican Immigration in Interdisciplinary Perspectives.* Cambridge, Mass.: David Rockefeller Center for Latin American Studies and Harvard University Press, pp. 207–221.

Earls, Felton. 1997. As quoted in "Tighter, Safer Neighborhoods." *Harvard Magazine* November/December.

Edmonston, B., and Jeffrey S. Passel. 1994. *Immigration and Ethnicity: The Integration of America's Newest Arrivals.* Washington, D.C.: Urban Institute Press.

Eisenstadt, T. A., and C. L. Thorup. 1994. *Caring Capacity vs. Carrying Capacity: Community Responses to Mexican Immigration in San Diego's North County.* La Jolla: Center for U.S.-Mexican Relations, University of California, San Diego.

Erikson, Erik. 1963. *Childhood and Society.* New York: W. W. Norton.

Eschbach, K., Jaqueline Hagan, and Nestor Rodriguez. 1997. *Death at the Border.* Houston: Center for Immigration Research.

Espenshade, Thomas J., and Maryanne Belanger. 1998. "Immigration and Public Opinion." In Marcelo M. Suárez-Orozco, ed., *Crossings: Mexican Immigration in Interdisciplinary Perspectives.* Cambridge, Mass.: David Rockefeller Center for Latin American Studies and Harvard University Press, pp. 365–403.

Espin, Olivia. 1987. "Psychological Impact of Migration on Latinas: Implications for Psychotherapeutic Practice." *Psychology of Women Quarterly* 11: 489–503.

——— 1999. *Women Crossing Boundaries: A Psychology of Immigration and Tranformations of Sexuality.* New York: Routledge.

Falicov, Celia Jaes. 1998. *Latino Families in Therapy: A Guide to Multicultural Practice.* New York: Guilford Press.

Fierman, Jaclyn. 1994. "Is Immigration Hurting the U.S.?" In N. Mills, ed., *Arguing Immigration.* New York: Simon & Schuster, pp. 67–75.

First, Joan, and John Wilshire Carrera. 1988. *New Voices: Students in U.S. Immigrant Public Schools.* Boston: National Coalition of Advocates for Students.

Flaskerud, J. H., and R. Uman. 1996. "Acculturation and Its Effects on Self-Esteem among Immigrant Latina Women." *Behavioral Medicine* 22: 123–133.

Fordham, Signithia. 1996. *Blacked Out: Dilemmas of Race, Identity, and Success at Capital High.* Chicago: University of Chicago Press.

Fordham, Signithia, and John Ogbu. 1986. "Black Students' Success: Coping with the Burden of Acting White." *Urban Review* 18, no. 3: 176–202.

Francese, Peter. 1994. "Aging America Needs Foreign Blood." In N. Mills, ed., *Arguing Immigration.* New York: Simon & Schuster, pp. 85–89.

Freire, Paulo. 1995. *Pedagogy of the Oppressed.* New York: Continuum.

Friedman, Lawrence J. 1999. *Identity's Architect: A Biography of Erik H. Erikson.* New York: Scribner.

Fritsch, Jane. 1993. "Smuggled to New York." *New York Times,* June 7, p. A1.

Fuligini, Andrew. 1997. "The Academic Achievement of Adolescents from Immigrant Families: The Roles of Family Background, Attitudes, and Behavior." *Child Development* 69, no. 2: 351–363.

Gándara, Patricia. 1994. "The Impact of the Educational Reform Movement on Limited English Proficient Students." In B. McLeod, ed., *Language and Learning: Educating Linguistically Diverse Students.* Albany: State University of New York Press.

——— 1995. *Over the Ivy Walls: The Educational Mobility of Low Income Chicanos.* Albany: State University of New York Press.

Gans, Herbert J. 1999. "Filling in Some Holes: Six Areas of Needed Immigration Research." *American Behavioral Scientist* 42: 1302–1313.

Garcia-Coll, Cynthia, and K. Magnuson. 1998. "The Psychological Experience of Immigration: A Developmental Perspective." In A. Booth, A. Crouter, and N. Landale, eds., *Immigration and the Family: Research and Policy on U.S. Immigrants.* Mahwah, N.J.: Lawrence Erlbaum, pp. 91–131.

Garcia-Coll, Cynthia, Janet Surrey, and Kathy Weingarten, eds. 1998. *Mothering against the Odds: Diverse Voices of Contemporary Mothers.* New York: Guilford Press.

Geertz, Clifford. 1973. *The Interpretation of Cultures.* New York: Basic Books.

Gibson, Margaret. 1988. *Accommodation without Assimilation: Sikh Immigrants in an American High School.* Ithaca, N.Y.: Cornell University Press.

——— 1997. "Complicating the Immigrant / Involuntary Minority Typology." *Anthropology and Education Quarterly* 28, no. 3: 431–454.

Gibson, Margaret, and John Ogbu, eds. 1991. *Minority Status and Schooling: A Comparative Study of Immigrant and Involuntary Minorities.* New York: Garland Press.

Glazer, N., and D. P. Moynihan. 1970. *Beyond the Melting Pot.* Cambridge, Mass.: MIT Press.

Goodenow, C., and O. Espin. 1993. "Identity Choices in Immigrant Adolescent Females." *Adolescence* 28, no. 109: 173–184.

Gordon, Milton. 1964. *Assimilation and American Life.* New York: Oxford University Press.

Grinberg, Leon, and Rebeca Grinberg, 1989. *Psychoanalytic Perspectives on Migration and Exile.* New Haven: Yale University Press.

Guarnizo, Luis. 1994. "Los Dominicanyork: The Making of a Binational Society." *Annals of the American Academy of Political and Social Science* 533: 70–86.

Gutierrez, David G. 1998. "Ethnic Mexicans and the Transformation of 'American' Social Space: Reflections on Recent History." In M. Suárez-Orozco, ed., *Crossings: Mexican Immigration in Interdisciplinary Perspectives.* Cambridge, Mass.: David Rockefeller Center for Latin American Studies and Harvard University Press, pp. 307–335.

Handlin, Oscar. 1951. *The Uprooted.* Boston: Little, Brown.

Hayes-Bautista, David, et al., 1988. *The Burden of Support: Young Latinos in an Aging Society.* Stanford, Calif.: Stanford University Press.

Heller, K., and R. W. Swindle. 1983. "Social Networks, Perceived Social Support, and Coping with Stress." In R. D. Felner, ed., *Preventative Psychology: Theory, Research, Practice in Community Intervention.* New York: Penguin.

Helms, Janet. 1990. *Black and White Racial Identity: Theory, Research, and Practice.* Westport, Conn.: Greenwood Press.

Hernandez, D., and Evan Charney, eds. 1998. *From Generation to Generation: The Health and Well-Being of Children in Immigrant Families.* Washington, D.C.: National Academy Press.

Heubert, Jay, ed. 1999. *Law and School Reform: Six Strategies for Promoting Educational Equity.* New Haven: Yale University Press.

Higham, John. 1975. *Send These to Me: Jews and Other Immigrants in Urban America.* New York: Atheneum.

———— 1980. *Strangers in the Land: Patterns of American Nativism, 1860–1925.* New Brunswick, N.J.: Rutgers University Press.

Hing, Bill Ong. 1993. *The Making and Remaking of Asian America through Immigration Policy, 1850–1990.* Stanford, Calif.: Stanford University Press.

Hoffmann, Eva. 1989. *Lost in Translation: A Life in a New Language.* New York: Penguin.

Hondagneu-Sotelo, Pierrete. 1994. *Gendered Transitions: Mexican Experiences of Immigration.* Berkeley: University of California Press.

Horowitz, Ruth. 1986. *Honor and the American Dream: Culture and Identity in a Chicano Community.* New Brunswick, N.J.: Rutgers University Press.

House, J. S. 1974. "Occupational Stress and Coronary Heart Disease: A Review." *Journal of Health and Social Behavior* 15: 12–27.

Huddle, Donald. 1993. "The Costs of Immigration." Released by Carrying Capacity Network, Houston.

Huerta, Teresa. 1998. "A Humanizing Pedagogy: Effective Instructional Practices for Latino Students." Qualifying paper, Graduate School of Education, Harvard University.

Hughes, Sarah. 1999. "Young Latinos Follow the American Dream." M.A. thesis, University of California, Berkeley.

Human Rights Watch. 1997. *Slipping through the Cracks: Unaccompanied Children Detained by the U.S. Immigration and Naturalization Service.* New York: Human Rights Watch.

———— 1998. *Locked Away: Immigration Detainees in Jails in the United States* 10, no. 1: 6.

"Immigrants Learn the Law: Easing Clash of Cultures." 1999. *New York Daily News,* April 1, p. 1.

"Immigration: Concerns Rising." 1994. *New York Times,* January 2, p. A3.

"Immigration Agency Weighs Changes in Citizenship Test." 1999. *New York Times,* July 5, p. A6.

Jacob, E., and C. Jordan. 1987. "Explaining the School Performance of Minority Students." *Anthropology and Education Quarterly* 18, no. 4.

Johnson, Diane. 1997. *Le Divorce*. New York: Dutton.

Kachru, B. B. 1994. "Paradigms of Marginality." Paper presented at the Teachers of English to Speakers of Other Languages annual conference, Baltimore, Md. March.

Kagan, Jerome, Anthony Appiah, and Gil Noam. 1988. "Identity." Unpublished manuscript. Cambridge, Mass.: Harvard Project on Schooling of Children.

Kao, G., and M. Tienda. 1995. "Optimism and Achievement: The Educational Performance of Immigrant Youth." *Social Science Quarterly* 76, no. 1: 1–19.

Khoury, Elizabeth, George Warheit, Rick Zimmerman, William Vega, and Andres Gil. 1999. "Gender and Ethnic Differences in the Prevalence of Alchohol, Cigarette, and Illicit Drug Use over Time in a Cohort of Young Hispanic Adolescents in South Florida." *Women and Health* 24, no. 1: 21–40.

LaFromboise, Teresa, Hardin Coleman, and Jennifer Gerton. 1998. "Psychological Impact of Biculturalism: Evidence and Theory." In P. B. Organista, K. Chun, and G. Martin, eds., *Readings in Ethnic Psychology*. New York: Routledge.

Landale, N. S., and R. S. Oropesa. 1995. "Immigrant Children and the Children of Immigrants: Inter- and Intra-Ethnic Group Differences in the United States." Population Research Group (PRG) Research Paper 95–2. East Lansing, Mich.: Institute for Public Policy and Social Research.

Laosa, L. 1989. *Psychological Stress, Coping, and the Development of the Hispanic Immigrant Child*. Princeton, N.J.: Educational Testing Service.

Lazarus, R. S., and S. Folkman. 1984. *Stress, Appraisal, and Coping*. New York: Springer.

Levitt, Peggy. 1996. "Transnationalizing Civil and Political Change: The Case of Transnational Organizational Ties between Boston and the Dominican Republic." Ph.D. diss., Massachusetts Institute of Technology.

———— 1997. "Future Allegiances: The Social and Political Implications of Transnationalism." Paper presented at the David Rockefeller Center for Latin American Studies, Harvard University, Cambridge, Mass. June 6.

Lieberson, Stanley, Guy Dalto, and Mary Ellen Johnson. 1975. "The Course of Mother Tongue Diversity in Nations." *American Journal of Sociology* 81: 34–61.

Lucas, T., R. Henze, and R. Donato. 1990. "Promoting the Success of Latino Language-Minority Students: An Exploratory Study of Six High Schools." *Harvard Educational Review* 60: 315–340.

Mahler, Sarah J. 1999. "Engendering Transnational Migration: A Case Study of Salvadorans." *American Behavioral Scientist,* 42, no. 4.

Maira, Sunaina. 1998. "The Quest for Ethnic Authenticity: Second-Generation Indian Americans in New York City." Ed.D. diss., School of Education, Harvard University.

Marcia, J. 1966. "Development and Validation of Ego-Identity Status." *Journal of Personality and Social Psychology* 3: 551–558.

Massey, Douglas, and Nancy Denton. 1993. *American Apartheid.* Cambridge, Mass.: Harvard University Press.

Millman, Joel. 1997. *The Other Americans: How Immigrants Renew Our Country, Our Economy, and Our Values.* New York: Viking.

Min, Pyong Gap. 1998. *Changes and Conflicts: Korean Immigrant Families in New York.* Boston: Allen and Bacon.

Minicucci, C., and Laurie Olsen. 1992. *Programs for Secondary Limited Proficient Students: A California Study.* Washington, D.C.: National Clearing House for Bilingual Education.

Moll, Luis. 1988. "Educating Latino Students." *Language Arts* 64: 315–324.

Molyneux, Maxine. 1999. "The Politics of the Cuban Diaspora in the United States." In Victor Bulmer-Thomas and James Dunkerley, eds., *The United States and Latin America: The New Agenda.* Cambridge, Mass.: David Rockefeller Center for Latin American Studies and Harvard University Press.

Moya, José C. 1998. *Cousins and Strangers: Spanish Immigrants in Buenos Aires, 1850–1930.* Berkeley: University of California Press.

Murnane, Richard. 1996. *Teaching the New Basic Skills: Principles for Educating Children to Thrive in a Changing Economy.* New York: Martin Kessler Books, Free Press.

Myers, Dowell. 1998. "Dimensions of Economic Adaptation by Mexican Origin Men." In Marcelo M. Suárez-Orozco, ed., *Crossings: Mexican Immigration in Interdisciplinary Perspectives.* Cambridge, Mass.: David Rockefeller Center for Latin American Studies and Harvard University Press, pp. 157–200.

National Research Council. 1997. *The New Americans: Economic, Demographic and Fiscal Effects of Immigration.* Washington, D.C.: National Research Council.

———— 1998. *From Generation to Generation: The Health and Well-Being of Children in Immigrant Families.* Washington, D.C.: National Academy Press.

Navarette, Jr., Ruben. 1993. *A Darker Shade of Crimson: Odyssey of a Harvard Chicano.* New York: Bantam.

Nelan, B. 1993. "Not Quite So Welcome Anymore." *Time,* September 21.

Nieto, S. 1996. *Affirming Diversity. 2d ed.* New York: Longman.

Ogbu, John. 1974. *The Next Generation: An Ethnography of Education in an Urban Neighborhood.* New York: Academic Press.

———— 1978. *Minority Education and Caste: The American System in Cross-Cultural Perspective.* New York: Academic Press.

Ogbu, John, and Maria Eugenia Matute-Bianchi. 1986. "Understanding Sociocultural Factors: Knowledge, Identity, and School Adjustment." In *Beyond Language: Social and Cultural Factors in the Schooling of Language Minority Students.* Sacramento: Bilingual Education Office, California State of Education.

Ogbu, John, and Herbert Simons. 1998. "Voluntary and Involuntary Minorities: A Cultural-Ecological Theory of School Performance with Some Implications for Education." *Anthropology and Education Quarterly* 29: 155–188.

Olneck, M. R., and M. Lazerson. 1974. "The School Achievement of Immigrant Children: 1899–1930. *History of Education Quarterly* 14: 453–482.

Olsen, Laurie. 1988. *Crossing the Schoolhouse Border: Immigrant Students in the California Public Schools.* Oakland: California Tomorrow.

———— 1998. *Made in America: Immigrant Students in Our Public Schools.* New York: New Press.

O'Neill, Eugene. 1984. *Long Day's Journey into Night.* New Haven: Yale University Press.

Orfield, Gary. 1998. "Commentary." In Marcelo M. Suárez-Orozco, ed., *Crossings: Mexican Immigration in Interdisciplinary Perspectives.* Cambridge, Mass.: David Rockefeller Center for Latin American Studies and Harvard University Press.

Orfield, Gary, L. Chew, R. L. Green, H. Liddell, J. D. Ramirez, and G. Stephens. 1999. "Progress Made, Challenges Remaining in San Francisco School Desegregation." San Francisco: Report of the Consent Decree Advisory Committee to the Federal District Court.

Orfield, Gary, and John T. Yun. 1999. *Resegregation in American Schools.* Cambridge, Mass.: Civil Rights Project, Harvard University.

Padilla, A., Kathryn Lindholm, Andrew Chen, Richard Dúran, Kenji Hakuta, Walace Lambert, and G. Richard Tucker. 1991. "The English-Only Movement: Myth, Reality, and Implications for Psychology." *American Psychologist* 46, no. 2: 120–130.

Papademetriou, D. 1994. "Immigration's Effects on the U.S." *Interpreter Releases* 71, no. 1: 1–5.

Parham, T. 1989. "Cycles of Psychological Nigrescence." *Counseling Psychologist* 17, no. 2: 187–226.

Park, Robert. 1930. "Social Assimilation." In E. Seligman and A. Johnson, eds., *Encyclopedia of the Social Sciences.* New York: Macmillan.

Park, Robert, and E. Burgess. 1969. *Introduction to the Science of Sociology.* Chicago: University of Chicago Press.

Passel, Jeffrey. 1994. *Immigrants and Taxes: A Reappraisal of Huddle's "The Cost of Immigrants."* Washington, D.C.: Urban Institute.

Pearlin, L. I., and C. Schooler. 1978. "The Structure of Coping." *Journal of Health and Social Behavior* 19, no. 3: 2–21.

Peters, Enrique Dussel. 1998. "Recent Structural Changes in Mexico's Economy." In Marcelo M. Suárez-Orozco, ed., *Crossings: Mexican Immigration in Interdisciplinary Perspectives.* Cambridge, Mass.: David Rockefeller Center for Latin American Studies and Harvard University Press, pp. 53–74.

Phinney, Jean. 1990. "Ethnic Identity in Adolescents and Adults: A Review of the Literature." *Psychological Bulletin* 108, no. 3: 499–514.

——— 1998. "Ethnic Identity in Adolescents and Adults: Review of Research." In P. B. Organista, K. Chun, and G. Martin, eds., *Readings in Ethnic Psychology.* New York: Routledge.

Piore, Michael. 1971. *Birds of Passage: Migrant Labor and Industrial Societies.* New York: Cambridge University Press.

Portes, Alejandro. 1993. "The New Second Generation." Press Release, School of International Relations, Johns Hopkins University, Baltimore, Md. June 3.

——— 1996a. *The New Second Generation.* New York: Russell Sage.

——— 1996b. "Transnational Communities: Their Emergence and Significance in the Contemporary World-System." In R. P. Korzeniewics and W. C. Smith, eds., *Latin America and the World Economy.* Westport, Conn.: Greenwood Press.

——— 1997. "Immigration Theory for a New Century: Some Problems and Opportunities." *International Migration Review* 31: 799–825.

——— 1998. "Globalization: The Rise of Transnational Communities." Paper delivered at the David Rockefeller Center for Latin American Studies, Harvard University. April 2.

Portes, Alejandro, and Lingxin Hao. 1998. "E Pluribus Unum: Bilingualism and Loss of Language in the Second Generation." *Sociology of Education* 71: 269–294.

Portes, Alejandro, and Richard Schauffler. 1994. "Language and the Second Generation: Bilingualisim Yesterday and Today." *International Migration Review* 28, no.4: 640.

Portes, Alejandro, and Alex Stepick. 1993. *City on the Edge: The Transformation of Miami.* Berkeley: University of California Press.

Portes, Alejandro, and Min Zhou. 1993. "The Second Generation: Segmented Assimilation and Its Variants," *Annals of the American Academy* 530: 74–96.

Proposition 187. 1994. "Illegal Aliens. Ineligibility for Public Services. Verification and Reporting." Initiative Statute, State of California.

Proulx, Annie E. 1996. *Accordion Crimes.* New York: Scribner.

"Reno Names Two to Shape Up Citizen Process." 1997. *New York Times,* April 26, p. A4.

Rodríguez, Luís J. 1993. *Always Running: La Vida Loca; Gang Days in L.A.* New York: Touchstone.

Rodriguez, Richard. 1982. *Hunger of Memory: The Education of Richard Rodriguez.* New York: Bantam.

Rohter, Larry. 1993. "Revisiting Immigration and the Open-Door Policy." *New York Times,* September 19, p. A4.

Romanucci-Ross, L., and George De Vos. 1995. *Ethnic Identity: Creation, Conflict, and Accommodation,* 3d ed. Walnut Creek, Calif.: Alta Mira Press.

Rong, Xue Lan, and Judith Prissle. 1998. *Educating Immigrant Students: What We Need to Know to Meet the Challenge.* Thousand Oaks, Calif.: Corwin Press.

Roosens, Eugene. 1989. *Creating Ethnicity: The Process of Ethnogenesis.* Newbury Park, Calif.: Sage.

Rosenthal, R., and L. Jacobson. 1968. *Pygmalion in the Classroom: Teacher Expectations and Pupil's Intellectual Development.* New York: Holt, Rinehart, and Winston.

Rothstein, Richard. 1994. "Immigration Dilemmas." In N. Mills, ed., *Arguing Immigration.* New York: Simon and Schuster, pp. 55–57.

Rumbaut, Rubén. 1977. "Life Events, Change, Migration and Depression." In W. E. Fann, I. Karocan, A. D. Pokorny, and R. L. Williams, eds., *Phenomenology and Treatment of Depression.* New York: Spectrum.

——— 1995. "The New Californians: Comparative Research Findings on the Educational Progress of Immigrant Children." In R. Rúmbaut and W. Cornelius, eds., *California's Immigrant Children.* La Jolla, Calif.: Center for U.S.-Mexican Studies, pp. 46–48.

——— 1996a. "Becoming American: Acculturation, Achievement, and Aspirations among Children of Immigrants." Paper presented at the Annual Meeting of the American Association for the Advancement of Science, Baltimore, Md. February 10.

——— 1996b. "Ties That Bind: Immigration and Immigrant Families in the United States." In Alan Booth, Ann C. Crouter, and Nancy Landale, eds., *Immigration and the Family: Research and Policy on U.S. Immigrants.* Mahwah, N.J.: Lawrence Erlbaum.

——— 1997. "Achievement and Ambition among Children of Immigrants in Southern California." Paper presented to the Jerome Levy Economics Institute of Bard College, Annandale-on-the-Hudson, New York.

Rumbaut, Rubén, and Wayne Cornelius, eds. 1995. *California's Immigrant Children: Theory, Research, and Implications for Educational Policy.* La Jolla, Calif.: Center for US-Mexican Studies.

Sachs, Susan. 1999. "Pressed by Backlog, U.S. Rethinks Citizenship Test." *New York Times,* July 5, p. A1.

Sanger, David. 1999. "Big Racial Disparity Persists in Internet Use." *New York Times,* July 9, p. A6.

Santiago, Esmeralda. 1998. *Almost a Woman.* Reading, Mass.: Perseus Books.

Saxenian, AnnaLee. 1999. *Silicon Valley's New Immigrant Entrepeneurs.* San Francisco: Public Policy Institute of California.

Schlossberg, Nancy K. 1984. *Counseling Adults in Transition: Linking Practice with Theory.* New York: Springer.

Seligman, Martin. 1990. *Learned Optimism.* New York: Pocket Books.

———— 1998. "The American Way of Blame," *APA Monitor* 29, no. 7.

"Seven Thais Enter Guilty Pleas For Detention in Sweatshop." 1996. *New York Times,* February 11, p. A39.

Sexton, Joe. 1997. "Captive in Queens." *New York Times,* July 22, p. A1.

Shuval, J. 1980. "Migration and Stress." in I. L. Kutasshm, L. B. Schlessinger, et al., *Handbook on Stress and Anxiety: Contemporary Knowledge, Theory, and Treatment.* San Francisco: Jossey-Bass.

Simon, Julian. 1989. *The Economic Consequences of Immigration.* Oxford: Basil Blackwell.

———— 1995. *Immigration: The Demographic and Economic Facts.* Washington, D.C.: The Cato Institute and National Immigration Forum.

Simon, Rita J. 1985. *Public Opinion and the Immigrant: Print Media Coverage, 1880–1980.* Lexington, Mass.: Lexington Books.

Simon, Rita J., and Susan H. Alexander. 1993. *The Ambivalent Welcome: Print Media, Public Opinion, and Immigration.* Westport, Conn.: Praeger.

Sluzki, Carlos. 1979. "Migration and Family Conflict." *Family Process* 18, no. 4: 379–390.

Smajkic, A., and S. Weane. 1995. "Special Issues of Newly Arrived Refugee Groups." In Susan Somach, ed., *Issues of War Trauma and Working with Refugees: A Compilation of Resources.* Washington, D.C.: Center for Applied Linguistics Refugee Service Center.

Smart, J. F., and D. W. Smart. 1995. "Acculturation Stress of Hispanics: Loss and Challenge." *Journal of Counseling and Development* 75: 390–396.

Smith, Robert. 1999. "The Education and Work Mobility of Second-Generation Mexican Americans in New York City: Preliminary Reflections on the Role of Gender, Ethnicity, and School Structure." Paper presented at the Eastern Sociological Society Meeting, Boston. March.

Snow, Catherine. 1993. "Bilingualisim and Second Language Acquisition." In Jean Berko Gleason and Nan Bernstein Ratner, eds, *Psycholinguistics*. Fort Worth, Tex.: Hartcourt Brace, pp. 392–416.

––––––– 1997. "The Myths around Being Bilingual." *Boston Globe*, July 13.

Somach, Susan. 1995. *Issues of War Trauma and Working with Refugees: A Compilation of Resources*. Washington, D.C.: Center for Applied Linguistics Refugee Service Center.

Sommer, Doris. 1999. *Aesthetics of Bilingualism*. Unpublished manuscript, Department of Romance Languages, Harvard University.

Steele, Claude. 1997a. "Stereotypes and Intellectual Identity." Lecture delivered at Harvard Graduate School of Education Forum. April 11.

––––––– 1997b. "A Threat in the Air: How Stereotypes Shape Intellectual Identity and Performance." *American Psychologist* 52, no. 6: 613–629.

Steinberg, Lawrence, B. Bradford Brown, and Sanford Dornbusch. 1996. *Beyond the Classroom: Why School Reform Has Failed and What Parents Need to Do*. New York: Simon and Schuster.

Stepick, Alex. 1998. *Pride against Prejudice: Haitians in the United States*. Boston: Allyn Bacon.

Stonequist, E. V. 1937. *The Marginal Man: A Study in Personality and Cultural Conflict*. New York: Scribners.

Suárez-Orozco, Carola. 1998. "The Transitions of Immigration: How Are They Different for Women and Men?" *David Rockefeller Center for Latin American Studies News*, Harvard University. Winter.

Suárez-Orozco, Carola, and Marcelo M. Suárez-Orozco. 1995. *Transformations: Migration, Family Life, and Achievement Motivation among Latino Adolescents*. Stanford, Calif.: Stanford University Press.

Suárez-Orozco, Marcelo M. 1989. *Central American Refugees and U.S. High Schools: A Psychosocial Study of Motivation and Achievement*. Stanford, Calif.: Stanford University Press.

––––––– 1994. "Anxious Neighbors: Belgium and Its Immigrant Minorities." In Wayne A. Cornelius, Philip L. Martin, and James F. Hollifield, eds., *Controlling Immigration: A Global Perspective*. Stanford, Calif.: Stanford University Press.

––––––– 1996. "Unwelcome Mats." *Harvard Magazine* 98, no. 6: 32–35.

––––––– 1998. *Crossings: Mexican Immigration in Interdisciplinary Perspectives*. Cambridge, Mass.: David Rockefeller Center for Latin American Studies and Harvard University Press.

––––––– 1999. "Latin American Immigration to the United States," in Victor Bulmer-Thomas and James Dunkerley, eds., *The United States and Latin America: The New Agenda*. Cambridge, Mass.: David Rockefeller

Center for Latin American Studies and Harvard University Press.

Suárez-Orozco, Marcelo M., and Antonius C. G. M. Robben. 2000. "Interdisciplinary Perspectives on Violence and Trauma." In Antonius C. G. M. Robben and Marcelo M. Suárez-Orozco, eds., *Cultures under Siege: Collective Violence and Trauma*. Cambridge: Cambridge University Press.

Suárez-Orozco, Marcelo M., Peter D. Roos, and Carola Suárez-Orozco. 1999. "Cultural, Educational, and Legal Perspectives on Immigration: Implications for School Reform." In Jay P. Hubert, ed., *Law and School Reform*. New Haven: Yale University Press, pp. 160–204.

Suro, R. 1998. *Strangers among Us: How Latino Immigration Is Transforming America*. New York: Alfred Knopf, pp. 13.

Takaki, Ronald. 1989. *Strangers from a Different Shore*. Boston: Little, Brown.

Tatum, Beverly. 1992. "Talking about Race, Learning about Racism: The Application of Racial Identity Development Theory to the Classroom. *Harvard Educational Review* 62, no. 1: 1–24.

———— 1997. *"Why Are All the Black Kids Sitting Together in the Cafeteria?" And Other Conversations about Race*. New York: Basic Books.

Taylor, Charles, 1994. "The Politics of Recognition." In Amy Gutman, ed., *Multiculturalism: Examining the Politics of Recognition*. Princeton, N.J.: Princeton University Press.

Tharp, Roland, and Ronald Gallimore. 1988. *Rousing Minds to Life: Teaching, Learning, and Schooling in Social Context*. New York: Cambridge University Press.

Trejo, Frank. 1999. "Hard Lesson." *Dallas Morning News,* January 27, p. A1.

Triandis, Harry. 1989. "The Self and Social Behavior in Differing Cultural Contexts." *Psychological Review* 96: 506–520.

Trueba, Henry. 1989. *Raising Silent Voices: Educating the Linguistic Minorities for the Twenty-first Century*. New York: Newbury.

Tsuda, Takeyuki. 1996. "Strangers in the Ethnic Homeland." Ph.D. diss., University of California at Berkeley.

Tyler, John, Richard J. Murnane, and Frank Levy. 1995. *Are Lots of College Graduates Taking High School Jobs? A Reconsideration of the Evidence*. Cambridge, Mass.: National Bureau of Economic Research.

Urrea, Luis Alberto. 1998. *Nobody's Son*. Tuscon: University of Arizona Press, p. 41.

Valdéz, Guadalupe. 1998. "The World Outside and Inside Schools: Language and Immigrant Children." *Educational Researcher* 27, no. 6: 9.

Valenzuela, A. 1999. "Gender Roles and Settlement Activities among

Children and Their Immigrant Families." *American Behavioral Scientist* 42, no. 4: 720–742.

Vigil, Diego. 1988. *Barrio Gangs: Street Life and Identity in Southern California.* Austin: University of Texas Press.

Villareal, José A., *Pocho.* 1959. New York: Anchor Books, pp. 149–150.

Volkan, V. D. 1993. "Immigrants and Refugees: A Psychodynamic Perspective," *Mind and Human Interaction* 4, no. 2: 63–69.

Vygotsky, L. S. 1978. *Mind in Society: The Development of Higher Psychological Processes.* Ed. and trans. M. Cole, V. John-Steiner, S. Scribner, and E. Souberman. Cambridge, Mass.: Harvard University Press.

Wagner, D. A., and R. L. Venezky. 1999. "Adult Literacy: The Next Generation." *Educational Researcher* 28, no. 1: 21–29.

Waldinger, Roger. 1997a. "Black-Immigrant Competition Re-Assessed: New Evidence from Los Angeles." Paper delivered at the David Rockefeller Center for Latin American Studies, Harvard University, Cambridge, Mass. April 7.

———— 1997b. "Social Capital or Social Closures? Immigrant Networks in the Labor Market." Working Paper Series 26. Lewis Center for Regional Policy Studies, University of California, Los Angeles.

Waldinger, Roger, and Mehdi Bozorgmehr, eds. 1996. *Ethnic Los Angeles.* New York: Russell Sage Foundation.

"Wanted: American Physicists." 1999. *New York Times,* July 23, p. A27.

Waters, Mary C. 1990. *Ethnic Options: Choosing Identities in America.* Berkeley: University of California Press.

———— 1997. "The Impact of Racial Segregation on the Education and Work Outcomes of Second-Generation West Indians in New York City." Paper presented to the Levy Institute Conference on the Second Generation, Bard College. October 25.

———— 1999. *Black Identities: West Indian Dreams and American Realities.* Cambridge, Mass.: Harvard University Press.

Waters, Tony. 1999. *Crime and Immigrant Youth.* Thousand Oaks, Calif.: Sage.

Weber, Max. 1968. *The City.* Trans. and ed. by Don Martindale. New York: Free Press.

Weld, Susan R., and William F. Weld. 1996. "We Should Always Lift Our Lamp to the World." *Boston Globe,* January 11, p. A28.

Wheaton, B. 1983. "Stress, Personal Coping Resources, and Psychiatric Symptoms: An Investigation of Interactive Models." *Journal of Health and Social Behavior* 24, no. 9: 208–229.

Williamson, Chilton, Jr. 1996. *The Immigration Mystique.* New York: Basic Books.

Wills, T. A. 1985. "Supportive Functions of Interpersonal Relationships." In

S. Cohen and S. L. Syme, eds., *Social Support and Health.* Orlando, Fla.: Academic Press.

Wilson, William. 1997. *When Work Disappears: The World of the New Urban Poor.* New York: Vintage Books.

Winnicott, D. W. 1971. *Playing and Reality.* Middlesex, Eng.: Penguin.

Wolf, Daniel H. 1988. *Undocumented Aliens and Crime: The Case of San Diego County.* La Jolla: Center for U.S.-Mexican Studies, University of California, San Diego.

Wong-Fillmore, L. 1991. "When Learning a Language Means Losing the First." *Early Childhood Research Quarterly* 6: 323–346.

Zentella, Ana Celia. 1997. *Growing Up Bilingual: Puerto-Rican Children in New York.* Oxford, Eng.: Blackwell.

Zéphir, Flore. 1996. *Haitian Immigrants in Black America: A Sociological and Sociolinguistic Portrait.* Westport, Conn.: Bergin and Garvey.

Zhou, Min. Forthcoming. "Second-Generation Fate: Progress, Decline, Stagnation?" In Roger Waldinger, ed., *Strangers at the Gate: New Immigrants in Urban America.* Berkeley: University of California Press.

Zhou, Min, and Carl L. Bankston III. 1998. *Growing Up American: How Vietnamese Children Adapt to Life in the United States.* New York: Russell Sage Foundation.

51 - assimilation
64 - Latino
70 - Zyda
84 85 Zyda

92 93 Zyda
98